ET 30889

# The Sino-Indian Border in Ladakh

# The Sino-Indian Borde

**ASIAN PUBLICATIONS SERIES**

**1** THE PHILOSOPHICAL LETTERS
OF WANG YANG-MING
*translated and annotated by Julia Ching*

**2** THE UIGHUR EMPIRE
ACCORDING TO THE T'ANG DYNASTIC HISTORIES
A Study in Sino-Uighur Relations 744–840
*translated and edited by Colin Mackerras*

**3** THE SINO-INDIAN BORDER IN LADAKH
*by Alastair Lamb*

in Ladakh  *Alastair Lamb*

UNIVERSITY OF SOUTH CAROLINA PRESS
*Columbia, South Carolina*

© *Alastair Lamb 1973*

*First American Edition 1975*

This book is copyright. Apart from any fair dealing for the purposes of private study, research, criticism, or review as permitted under the Copyright Act, no part may be reproduced by any process without written permission. Inquiries should be made to the Australian National University Press.

*Published 1973 in the Commonwealth of Australia by*
AUSTRALIAN NATIONAL UNIVERSITY PRESS
Canberra, A.C.T.

*Published 1975 in the United States of America by*
UNIVERSITY OF SOUTH CAROLINA PRESS
Columbia, S.C.

*Manufactured in the United States of America*

**Library of Congress Cataloging in Publication Data**

Lamb, Alastair, 1930–
    The Sino-Indian border in Ladakh.

    (Asian publications series, no. 3)
    1. India—Boundaries—China. 2. China—Boundaries—India. 3. Ladakh—Boundaries. I. Title.
DS450.C5L33    1974         341.42′09546        73–19964
ISBN 0-87249-300-8

# Preface

In 1962, while the Chinese and Indians were adopting postures which could only lead to some kind of armed conflict, I was working on the British archives in the Public Record Office and the India Office Library in London, my main interest at that time being the origins of the McMahon Line, the Indo-Tibetan border along the Assam Himalaya, although I also devoted some attention to the history of the Ladakh border with a view to writing about it at length at some later date. Subsequently, with the publication in 1963 of Dr Alder's admirable *British India's Northern Frontier 1865-95*,[1] I felt that the history of British relations with Ladakh and their interest in the Karakoram mountains up to 1895 had been so well covered as not to require another detailed study. In writing the relevant sections of my *The China-India Border*[2] I found Alder's work, which I first saw in Ph.D thesis form in the library of the University of Bristol, extremely useful. Alder's study, however, comes to an end in 1895, a date which does not coincide with any final solution of boundary problems in Ladakh and the Karakoram, though it does mark the effective end of Anglo-Russian crises arising from disputes over the alignment of the Russo-Afghan border in the Pamirs. I decided, accordingly, to concentrate my research

[1] London 1963.
[2] *The China-India Border: the origins of the disputed boundaries*, Chatham House Essays No. 2, London 1964.

on the period after 1895 while I was working as a Senior Fellow in History in the Research School of Social Sciences of the Australian National University from 1964 to 1966. The result was the two papers in this monograph and the maps which accompany them. Since this work was carried out in Canberra, it gave me great pleasure to accept Professor Wang Gungwu's suggestion that it should now be published in Canberra.

The history of border tracts, particularly those situated in remote areas, cannot be elucidated to any degree of satisfaction without the proper use of maps. A number of the major historical controversies to have emerged from the Sino-Indian border dispute, for example, would perhaps assume a rather different aspect if the disputants involved were more familiar with the terrain about which they have argued. In my study of the Sino-Indian border in Ladakh and along the Karakoram I endeavoured to plot as many significant features as I could on maps and to compare old and new cartographical ideas by this method in order to see whether apparent changes in border alignment might reflect no more than improvements in the accuracy of topographical survey. While in Canberra I drew nearly a hundred maps of one kind or another in this study: twenty-one of them are reproduced here.

I would like to thank Sir Keith Hancock and the Department of History of the Research School of Social Sciences in the Australian National University who provided me with drawing board, stencils and a wide variety of special drafting equipment not usually employed by the orthodox historian. I also owe a debt here to Professor O. H. K. Spate who gave me much encouragement in some of my more experimental map drawing. Finally I must express my gratitude for the way in which the photographic section of the John Curtin School of Medical Research of the Australian National University made reductions for purposes of reproduction of my original large-scale drawings. For any defects in the maps themselves, of course, I am alone responsible. The maps, which appear at the end of this monograph, are referred to in the text: some of them, however, require more than a short caption and are accompanied by a commentary.

The first of the two papers which make up this monograph has never before appeared in print though it was presented in a cyclostyled version to delegates to the International Conference of Asian History held at the University of Hong Kong in late 1964. It was designed to meet certain criticisms which had just been raised against one of the maps (not drawn by myself in this instance) in my *The China-India Border*, and which have been raised since in connection with some passages in my *The McMahon Line*,[3] the chief critics

[3] London 1966.

being Drs S. Gopal, M. W. Fisher, and L. E. Rose. These persons, as well as Sir Olaf Caroe, would seem to have been persuaded by the far from disinterested view of Himalayan cartography of the Ministry of External Affairs of the Government of India: and, indeed, so much to official Indian taste were comments of this kind that an extremely hostile review by Sir Olaf Caroe of *The China-India Border* was actually reproduced and circulated by the Indian High Commission in Canberra.[4] The cartographical arguments, however, still stand; and I trust that my explanation as to why old maps are not always entirely reliable may yet be of interest.

At the time when these particular criticisms were made, of course, it was still fashionable to regard the Indians as the heroes and the Chinese as the villains, the men in black hats, in the Sino-Indian melodrama. There is a certain irony in the fact that the combination of the Vietnam War and President Nixon would seem to have produced a new attitude towards this kind of question. In 1964 to see any merit in the Chinese case vis-à-vis anything, was to invite the accusation of being, to quote Sir Olaf Caroe, 'brainwashed by Moscow and Peking'. It is probable that today one would no longer run the risk of being charged with such strange mental gymnastics.

The major question raised in the paper, namely how the 1899 British note to the Chinese Government should have been so gravely misquoted by Mr Nehru in a formal communication with the Prime Minister of the Chinese People's Republic, and, incidentally, how the Chinese, who presumably still possessed the original text of the note, never brought themselves to point out the misquotation, still remains unanswered. Here is a matter which perhaps deserves further scholarly attention.

The second part of this monograph was written in Canberra in 1965. It was originally intended to form part of a larger work covering the history of British Indian relations with Sinkiang and the evolution of the Karakoram border over the

---

[4] Sir Olaf Caroe's critique appeared in the *Geographical Journal* in 1964. When the author pointed out to him the reasons why he had treated the 1899 boundary discussions as he did, Sir Olaf replied to the effect that it did not really matter what the facts of the case were—the important thing was that the British should support India as the Indian Republic was still very much part of the British heritage. One wonders what Sir Olaf's reaction would be were he now to witness a parade of the Indian armed forces: MIG aircraft can hardly be described as a positive contribution towards British exports.

Sir Olaf Caroe, it should be noted, was at one time Secretary to the Foreign Department of the Government of India; and, more than any man, he deserves to be regarded as the architect of the Sino-Indian border in the last years of the British Raj. For a most interesting study of Sir Olaf Caroe's own way of handling documentary material relating to the Sino-Indian border, see K. Gupta, 'The McMahon Line 1911-45: the British legacy', *The China Quarterly* XLVII, July/September 1971.

period 1895-1947. The section which was completed, while in a sense a fragment, has yet a certain validity in its own right as an account of the Raskam question and its wider implications for Anglo-Russian and Anglo-Chinese diplomacy.

The problem posed by the Mir of Hunza's claims to certain rights in Raskam and the Taghdumbash Pamir on the northern side of the main Karakoram waterparting resulted in the British boundary proposals to the Chinese Government of 1899. These proposals, the only formal definition of a border in this region that the British ever appear to have offered to China, still have relevance today not only to the understanding of the Sino-Indian boundary dispute in Ladakh but also to the settlement in 1963 of the Sino-Pakistani border along the western end of the Karakoram Range. Both these issues have their bearing on the present Indo-Pakistani confrontation. Without the Aksai Chin problem Sino-Indian relations might not have deteriorated to the extent they did in the climactic clash of late 1962. Without the settlement of the Sino-Pakistani border, which, as the reader will see, to some extent emerged out of the problem of the status of Hunza of which the Raskam crisis was in great measure a reflection, Pakistan might never have evolved today not only China's major ally on the littoral of the Indian Ocean but also a state in direct land contact with Chinese territory by a motor road through the Karakoram.[5]

ALASTAIR LAMB
University of Ghana
1972

[5] For a general picture of the region discussed in the second paper, with special references to the orientation of mountain ranges and watersheds, see Maps 4, 5, and 6.

# Contents

| | |
|---|---|
| Preface | v |
| List of maps | x |
| Introduction | 1 |
| I  Note on a problem of boundary definition in Ladakh | 5 |
| II  Aksai Chin and the Raskam crisis: boundary definition in the Karakoram, 1895-1907 | 17 |
| The strategic implications of the 1895 Pamirs settlement | 17 |
| Chinese thoughts on a Karakoram boundary | 29 |
| The Raskam crisis: first phase | 36 |
| The 1899 proposals to China | 42 |
| The Raskam crisis: second phase | 51 |
| The 1899 boundary: some later stages | 60 |
| Postscript | 69 |
| Maps | 75 |

# List of Maps

1. Sinkiang and its neighbours *76*
2. Sinkiang showing principal towns *77*
3. The western sector of the Sino-Indian boundary dispute, showing the relationship of the 1899 line to the modern Chinese roads and the present Indian-claimed border with Chinese territory in Tibet and Sinkiang *79*
4. Major watersheds in the Pamirs and the western end of the Karakoram *81*
5. Major watersheds in the eastern Karakoram and the western Kunlun *82*
6. Major watersheds in the Aksai Chin and Lingzitang plateaus *83*
7. The Aksai Chin and the plotting of the 1899 line: comparison between old and new maps *85*
8. Borders in the Aksai Chin area: a comparison of alignments from maps published in 1874, 1947, and 1950 *87*
9. A slightly simplified tracing of the map appended to the Simla Convention of 1914 and showing boundaries of Inner and Outer Tibet *89*
10. Comparison between the extreme north-western end of the red line in the 1914 Simla Convention map and the present Indian claim line in Ladakh along the Kunlun range *91*

## LIST OF MAPS

11  Three stages in the evolution of the territorial status of Aksai Chin in British and Indian eyes *93*

12  The Russo-Afghan border along the Oxus and the Wakhan tract *95*

13  Various boundary alignments in the Pamirs and the western Karakoram *97*

14  Various boundary alignments in the eastern Karakoram and the Kunlun *99*

15  Various boundary alignments in the Aksai Chin region *101*

16  Raskam and the Taghdumbash Pamir *103*

17  The western end of the 1899 line with 1905 modifications and compared with the 1963 line agreed between China and Pakistan *105*

18  A section of the north-eastern boundary of Ladakh as shown on a British map of the late 1840s *107*

19  Detailed map of the Aksai Chin region showing location of modern Chinese and Indian claims, the Chinese road between Sinkiang and Tibet, and the 1899 line *109*

20  Map showing some significant variations between Indian maps since 1954 and British maps relating to the boundaries along the Karakoram and the eastern side of Ladakh *111*

21  Johnson's map of the northern frontier of Kashmir, based on his journey to Khotan in 1865 *113*

# Introduction

In 1962 there took place what Neville Maxwell has described as 'India's China war'. The reasons for the deterioration of Sino-Indian relations that was such a feature of international history from the mid-1950s onward are many and complex. One, however, is simple enough. The border in Ladakh between India and Chinese territory, never adequately defined in the British period, became the subject of a dispute so acrimonious that even such a major clash of arms as took place in late 1962 has not sufficed to solve it.

The full story of how it was that British influence expanded during the nineteenth century through Kashmir State into the Karakoram Range and the fringes of the Pamirs has been told elsewhere, notably by Alder (to whom reference has already been made) and by Dorothy Woodman in her *Himalayan Frontiers*[1]; and for this reason a brief background summary should suffice here.

The key point is that the British approached the borders of Ladakh with both Tibet and Sinkiang through Kashmir; and from 1846, when the State of Jammu and Kashmir came under British paramountcy, right up to Partition in 1947, that State enjoyed a unique position in the British imperial structure.[2] The consequences of this fact were indeed to be far

---
[1] London 1969.
[2] I have discussed the origins of Kashmir and the British connection with that State in *Crisis in Kashmir*, London 1966.

reaching. On the one hand, out of it emerged the Indo-Pakistani Kashmir dispute which has never ceased to bedevil the relations between the two successor states to the British Raj. On the other hand, it contributed greatly to the ambiguities of the limits of Ladakh, which district, by virtue of its status as a Kashmiri province, the British showed a certain reluctance to treat as if it were part of directly administered British territory.

From the British point of view Kashmir was of interest in a number of respects, not least because the Vale provided a pleasant climate and the hills abounded with interesting game and attractive trekking routes. In the widest context of British imperial policy, however, the major significance of Kashmir lay in its role as a buffer between British India on the one hand and Chinese and Russian territory on the other. The mountainous regions through which ran the northern and northeastern borders of Kashmir were in themselves of little value, but they did at times appear to constitute a major barrier to the inexorable advance towards the Indian plains of the Tsarist (and later the Soviet) Empire. The need for such a barrier, and its theoretical shape, varied from time to time. So also did British concepts of exactly where the barrier should lie. When it seemed as if the Russians would take over Sinkiang (Chinese Turkestan), there were British strategists who advocated pushing the Kashmir border as far northwards as possible. At other periods the balance of opinion tended to favour a more moderate border, geographically speaking, with reliance being placed on Chinese control of Sinkiang as the major bar to Russian encroachment.[3] One consequence of these divergent views was that by 1947 the British had never come to any final decision as to which line they really wanted. The nearest they ever came to doing so and to communicating their ideas on the matter to their neighbours was in 1898 and 1899.

The evolution of the British border in northwestern India was a long and complicated process involving not only Kashmir but also Afghanistan and petty hill states like Chitral and Hunza. It was achieved partly by frontier campaigns, partly by negotiation with the indigenous rulers of the border tracts and partly through diplomacy in London, Peking, and St Petersburg. By 1895 most of the border had been settled on paper if not always actually demarcated on the ground. The Anglo-Russian agreement over the Pamirs in 1895 completed the definition of the border between Russia and Afghanistan, while the Durand agreement of 1893 defined with a few minor ambiguities the border between Afghanistan and British India (Map 13). Within this framework, as the Anglo-Russian Convention of 1907 was to recognise formally,

[3] For fluctuations in British ideas about the Ladakh border see Map 15.

Afghanistan became a true buffer between the British and Russian empires in Asia and ceased to be a bone of contention between them. The settling of the limits of Afghanistan also in practice resulted in the settling of the eastern limits of the Russian advance into the Pamirs, but this fact was not so clear in 1895 to several British strategists brought up in the old tradition of the 'Great Game'.

The 1895 Pamirs agreement contained one great omission from the British point of view. It did not set a limit to Russian progress eastwards in the Pamirs across the Sarikol Range into Sinkiang. Much of the border between Russian territory and Sinkiang had in fact been both delimited and demarcated in the 1880s, but one gap remained. Along the Sarikol Range, the watershed between the Oxus and the Tarim Basin, no Sino-Russian border existed. It had been a British hope that such a border would in fact emerge from the proceedings which resulted in the 1895 Pamirs agreement, but the Chinese refused to participate, probably because they considered that this agreement involved the surrender of rather nebulous Chinese claims to the west of the Sarikol Range.[4] It was theoretically possible, therefore, for the Russians to penetrate this gap, perhaps even with Chinese connivance, and extend their acquisitions in the Pamirs eastward right up to the limits of Tibet. Were this to happen, of course, the Russians would have outflanked Afghanistan and, directly touching Tibet, would threaten the entire central and eastern sectors of the northern frontier of India from Kashmir to Burma. To meet this possibility the British had two solutions. One was to see that Sinkiang, right up to the Sarikol Range, remained Chinese. The other was to secure a northern border in Kashmir so far to the north that it would, as it were, intersect the potential Russian line of advance. This second possibility, in fact, involved the exercise of British sovereignty over territory which the Chinese regarded as theirs, and in the event it was not adopted. The possibility, however, that it might be necessary to take under the British wing such territory effectively inhibited the British from the negotiation with China of a clearly defined Sino-British border in Kashmir following a more moderate, that is to say more southerly, line and involving no conflict with Chinese territorial claims. A border of this kind was almost achieved in 1899, but the British failed to press the Chinese hard enough to give birth to a formal border treaty. The lack of such a treaty is one of the elements which created the tragedy of the modern Sino-Indian dispute over the Aksai Chin.

[4] See Map 12. The space between B and C represents Chinese claims, to all intents and purposes lost in 1895, though some recent Chinese writers have persisted in maintaining that Chinese territory extends westwards in the Pamirs across the Sarikol range and includes Somatash and other points.

INTRODUCTION

As Neville Maxwell has recently shown in his *India's China War*[5], the Aksai Chin dispute has been of great importance to the Chinese in their attitude towards not only the Western Sector of the Sino-Indian border but to the fundamental shape of Sino-Indian relations. So long as the Aksai Chin question is unanswered the whole Sino-Indian issue, it can well be argued, remains unresolved. While the ultimate settlement of the pattern of relations between the nations of the subcontinent and their Chinese neighbour can, no doubt, be based only upon political factors, it is unlikely that anything like such a settlement can take place before the Sino-Indian border is defined to the satisfaction of both parties. In Ladakh the author has felt since 1962 that the line proposed to China by the British in 1899, the history of which forms the main theme of the two pieces published here, is the only viable basis for bilateral Sino-Indian discussion about actual delimitation and demarcation, because it is the only line in the key Aksai Chin region traversed by the Chinese road from Sinkiang to Western Tibet which has a proper diplomatic pedigree of any kind at all. On the whole, in its dealing with other neighbours since the Chinese Communist régime took power over twenty years ago Peking has shown a surprising measure of respect for boundary lines for which good precedents can be produced, even if those precedents date back to the bad old days of colonial empires and 'unequal treaties'.[6] As a contribution towards the understanding of the 1899 line, its background, even its whereabouts, not to mention its subsequent treatment by diplomats, the information contained in the following two pieces and the accompanying maps may still be of some value.

[5]London 1970. Maxwell's book, apart from being a highly readable account of a complex subject, is also probably unique in that it is the first reasonably objective account of the Sino-Indian border, maps and all, actually to have been published in India.

[6]I have discussed Chinese attitudes towards old treaties in a number of other publications. See, for example, 'China's Land Borders', *Australia's Neighbours*, Sept.-Oct. 1964; 'The Sino-Pakistani Boundary Agreement of 2 March 1963', *Australian Outlook*, Dec. 1964; 'Treaties, Maps and the Western Sector of the Sino-Indian Boundary Dispute', in J. G. Starke (ed.), *The Australian Year Book of International Law 1965*, Sydney, Melbourne, and Brisbane 1966; *Asian Frontiers*, London 1968; 'The Sino-Indian and Sino-Russian borders: some comparisons and contrasts', in J. Ch'en and N. Tarling (eds.), *Studies in the Social History of China and Southeast Asia*, Cambridge 1970.

# I Note on a problem of boundary definition in Ladakh

In March 1899 Sir Claude MacDonald, the British Minister at Peking, delivered a note to the Chinese Government in which was outlined a proposed definition of the Sino-Indian border from the Pamirs to Western Tibet at a point in the general region of longitude 80°E and latitude 34°30′N. This document, dated 14 March 1899, was, the published evidence would suggest, the only formal detailed statement of the alignment of the boundary in this quarter which an Indian Government ever caused to be communicated to a Chinese Government until the outbreak of the Sino-Indian boundary dispute in the 1950s. As such, it is clearly a document of some considerable interest. It concerns only a portion of the total length of the disputed border in Ladakh, but it is a section which includes the Aksai Chin region through which the Chinese have constructed a motor road linking Sinkiang to Tibet;[1] and many observers would agree that the struggle for possession of the Aksai Chin is the key to the whole crisis in Sino-Indian relations.[2]

The Indian Government of late has denied that the 1899

---

[1] For general maps of Sinkiang and its neighbours, including Tibet, see Maps 1 and 2. Maps 3 and 19 show the location of the Chinese road.
[2] Throughout this paper I use the term Aksai Chin to refer to what properly should be called West Aksai Chin, that portion of territory which the Indian Government at present maintains is located in the extreme northeast of Ladakh and the possession of which is now subject to Sino-Indian dispute.

note is particularly relevant to the boundary dispute. They informed the Chinese during the 1960-61 discussions that:

in 1899 the British did not propose to delimit the boundary between Ladakh and Kashmir on the one hand and Tibet on the other. As there had been some discussion regarding the status and rights of the ruler of Hunza, the British Government gave a description of the northern boundary of Kashmir with Sinkiang. It was stated explicitly in that context that the northern boundary ran along the Kuen Lun range to a point east of 80° Longitude, where it met the eastern boundary of Ladakh. This made it clear beyond doubt that the whole of the Aksai Chin area lay in Indian territory.[3]

These words, it should be noted, were no more than an amplification of the remarks which Mr Nehru addressed to Prime Minister Chou En-lai on 26 September 1959, when he noted that:

the proposal made in 1899 by the British Government referred not to the eastern frontier of Ladakh with Tibet but to the northern frontier of Ladakh and Kashmir with Sinkiang. It was stated in that context that the northern boundary ran along the Kuen Lun range to a point east of 80° east longitude, where it met the eastern boundary of Ladakh. This signified beyond doubt that the whole of Aksai Chin lay in Indian territory. The Government of China did not object to this proposal.[4]

[3]India, Ministry of External Affairs, *Report of the Officials of the Governments of India and the People's Republic of China on the Boundary Question*, White Paper No. I, New Delhi 1961, p. 55.
[4]India, Ministry of External Affairs, *Notes, Memoranda and Letters exchanged between the Governments of India and China, September-*

This interpretation of the 1899 note has been followed by many writers of late, including, for example, H. E. Richardson.[5] They have all, not having seen the original text of the note, stated that it contained a British claim to Aksai Chin.

In fact, however, it now transpires that the British note to the Chinese Government of 14 March 1899, far from declaring that Aksai Chin was British, actually admitted in precise terms that most of what is known as Aksai Chin in the terminology of the present Sino-Indian boundary dispute, including the territory through which, to judge from Indian published evidence, the main Chinese road between Sinkiang (Chinese Turkestan) and Tibet runs, should belong to China. This fact was first revealed by three American authors, Margaret W. Fisher, Leo E. Rose, and Robert A. Huttenback, who note in their *Himalayan Battleground: Sino-Indian rivalry in Ladakh* that by the boundary proposed in 1899 'most of the territory currently in dispute between Delhi and Peking [in Ladakh] would have been conceded to China'.[6]

*November 1959*, White Paper No. II, New Delhi 1959, p. 36.
[5]H. E. Richardson, *Tibet and Its History*, London 1962, p. 224.
[6]London 1963, p. 69. See also *Times Literary Supplement*, 2 Jan. 1964, front page article 'Peking and Delhi'. The present author, in fact, pointed out the true implications of the 1899 note to Dr Robert Huttenback whom he met by chance in the India Office Library in late 1962 after having been shown the original galleys of *Himalayan Battleground*. The galleys at this stage contained the Nehru version of the note and were then corrected.

The 1899 note was part of an attempt by Lord Elgin's Administration in India to secure an agreed Anglo-Chinese boundary from Afghanistan to Tibet. I have described the circumstances which resulted in its despatch in *The China-India Border*.[7] The 1899 note was based on a description of the boundary alignment which Lord Elgin sent to Lord George Hamilton, the Secretary of State for India, on 27 October 1898, and which gave the following alignment from the Karakoram Pass eastwards (it also dealt with the boundary westwards from the Karakoram Pass to the Afghan border, which need not concern us here):

from the Karakoram Pass the crests of the range run nearly east for about half a degree, and then turn south to a little below the 35th parallel of North Latitude. Rounding then what in our maps is shown as the source of the Karakash, the line of hills to be followed runs north-east to a point east of Kizil Jilga and from there, in a south-easterly direction, follows the Lak Tsung Range until that meets a spur running south from the Kuen Lun Range which has hitherto been shown on our maps as the eastern boundary of Ladakh. This is a little east of 80° East Longitude. We regret that we have no map to show the whole line either accurately or on a large scale.[8]

The note which Sir Claude MacDonald presented to the Chinese Government on 14 March 1899 repeated this description, with the additional comment that half a degree was the same as 100 *li*. MacDonald noted that:

it will not be necessary to mark out the frontier. The natural frontier is the crest of a range of mighty mountains, a great part of which is quite inaccessible. It will be sufficient if the two Governments [of Great Britain and China] . . . enter into an agreement to recognise the frontier as laid down by its clearly marked geographical features.[9]

The most casual reading of this boundary definition shows that it does *not* run, in contrast to what Mr Nehru suggested to Prime Minister Chou En-lai, from the Karakoram Pass due east along the Kunlun Range to a point east of 80°E longitude. The Kunlun Range runs roughly along the 36th parallel. The boundary in the MacDonald note for much of its length in the sector under consideration runs south of the 35th parallel. At this point at little east of 80°E longitude the boundary has long left the crest of the Kunlun Range, if indeed it ever ran along that range at all, and now meets 'a spur running south' from the Kunlun Range.

The boundary defined in the MacDonald note is based on 'clearly marked geographical features'.[10] What are these

[7] Op. cit., pp. 100-14.
[8] Ibid., p. 103.
[9] Ibid., p. 104. See Map 19 for the plotting of this line.

[10] Dr S. Gopal, who for some years directed the Historical Division of the Indian Ministry of External Affairs and who was in great measure responsible for the compilation of the Indian case in the Sino-Indian boundary dispute, has dismissed the 1899 line as 'an arbitrary line with no geographical or historical basis' (*Times Literary Supplement*, 6 Feb. 1964, letter from Dr S. Gopal).

features? From the Karakoram Pass to the point where it rounds 'what on our maps is shown as the source of the Karakash', there can be no doubt that the intended alignment follows the watershed between streams flowing into the Shyok River, a tributary of the Indus, and those flowing into the Karakash which runs northwards into the Tarim Basin. The next geographical features are not quite so clear; but there can be no serious doubt about them. From where it rounds the sources of the Karakash to the 'point east of Kizil Jilga' the line undoubtedly follows the watershed between the Karakash and streams running into the internal drainage system of the Tang Tso (lake). At the 'point east of Kizil Jilga' the line meets the Lak Tsung Range. This is not prominently marked on modern maps, but its course can be equated with the watershed between the Tang Tso Basin and the basin of the Amtogor Lake and the watershed between the Sarigh Jilganang Lake and the Amtogor Lake. The Lak Tsung Range comes to an end when it meets the watershed between the Sarigh Jilganang and Amtogor Lakes on the one hand, and the Nopte and Tsoggar Lakes on the other. This particular watershed is what the note clearly means by 'a spur running south from the Kunlun Range which has hitherto been shown on our maps as the eastern boundary of Ladakh'. The boundary follows this watershed southwards to the Lanak Pass at the head of the Changchenmo Valley.

In Map 6 of *The China-India Border*, I have shown this line of the 1899 note as I traced it out on the 1:1,000,000 G.S.G.S. map Asia N.I.44 (1949 edition). The eastern terminus of the 1899 line, thus delineated, is not shown at a point a little *east* of 80°E longitude; it is marked at a point a little *west* of 80°E longitude. Some Indian critics have not been slow to comment on this change.[11] Why is it that the 1899 line, when plotted on a good modern map, does not entirely agree with the verbal description given in Sir Claude MacDonald's note?

The answer to this question is simple enough. The maps of the northern parts of Ladakh which were available to the Indian Government in 1898 or 1899 were not remarkable for their accuracy. We have seen that in the definition of the boundary of 1898 Lord Elgin regrets the lack of accurate large scale maps. The basic survey of Ladakh was the Kashmir survey of the 1860s, the results of which were published in the *Kashmir Atlas* of 1868. For the Aksai Chin portion the Kashmir survey depended almost entirely on the work of W. H. Johnson who made a traverse of this region on a north-south axis in 1865. Johnson's survey, plane table not trigonometrical, was carried out in a hurry in extremely difficult conditions; and its defects are notorious. Yet it re-

[11] See, for example, *Times Literary Supplement*, 20 Feb. 1964, letter from Dr S. Gopal.

mained the basic source of cartographical information on the Aksai Chin and its neighbourhood for the rest of the nineteenth century. Johnson located a number of features further to the east than was in fact the case. His Sarigh Jilganang Lake, for example, has a stream flowing into it which rises in some mountains more than ten miles to the *east* of the 80th meridian; while on a modern map like the G.S.G.S. Asia 1:1,000,000 N.I.44 the eastern limit of the Sarigh Jilganang Basin is ten miles to the *west* of the 80th meridian. There is, thus, a shift eastward of some twenty miles of the Sarigh Jilganang Basin in the Johnson map as compared to modern maps.[12]

The errors of the Johnson survey of the Aksai Chin area, once made, persisted on into the twentieth century. They are to be seen clearly in the map at a scale of 16 miles to the inch, based on Trigonometrical Survey of India sources, which F. Drew included in his *Jummoo and Kashmir Territories*[13] and which I have drawn upon as one of the sources for Maps 8 and 15. The Royal Geographical Society map *Tibet and the Surrounding Regions*, at a scale of 60 miles to the inch, shows characteristic Johnson features, of which the eastward shift of the Sarigh Jilganang Basin and the peculiar heart-shaped form of Amtogor Lake are examples, in successive editions up to 1904; the 1906 edition has been corrected to compare closely with modern maps. A map published in 1908 by the Indian Foreign Department for use in connection with Aitchison's *Collection of Treaties*[14] still shows the Johnson eastward shift of the Sarigh Jilganang Basin. This map, 32 miles to the inch, Reg. No. 346 E., F.D.—Feb. 08.—670, is especially interesting in this context as it was intended to show a frontier alignment following the definition contained in the 1899 note.

This brief discussion of the history of the survey of Ladakh should suffice to show that while, on the maps then available, the frontier in the 1899 note would join the spur running south from the Kunlun Range at a point slightly east of the 80th meridian, if we trace that same alignment on a modern map we will find that this particular point falls to the west of the 80th meridian. The situation can be best appreciated by comparing the two maps printed side by side here as

---

[12]For the history of the Kashmir survey, see *China-India Border*, op. cit., Chapters 5 and 6. Johnson's map is printed as No. 13 in India, Ministry of External Affairs, *Atlas of the Northern Frontier of India*, New Delhi 1960. See also Maps 7 and 15 in this monograph. For W. H. Johnson's views of the Aksai Chin region and the correct alignment between Kashmiri and Chinese and Tibetan territory, see Map 21. This map is a simplified tracing of Johnson's own map as published by the Royal Geographical Society in W. H. Johnson, 'Report on his Journey to Ilchi, the capital of Khotan, in Chinese Tartary', *Journal of the Royal Geographical Society* XXXVII (1867).
[13]London 1875.
[14]Calcutta 1909.

Map 7. In the left hand map, which is based on the *Kashmir Atlas* and other sources, the watersheds followed by the 1899 alignment can be clearly observed to cross the 80th meridian; in the right hand map, which is traced from the G.S.G.S. Asia 1:1,000,000 sheet no. N.I.44, edition of 1949, the watersheds in question do not reach the 80th meridian at all. In both maps the junction of the 1899 alignment with the so called spur running south from the Kunlun (a somewhat nebulous feature in modern maps) is indicated by a heavy black arrow.

On the right hand of Map 7 it will be noted that, north of the 1899 alignment, two alternative courses for the present Indian-claimed boundary in the Aksai Chin are marked. This is a result of ambiguities in the description of that frontier which the Indian Government presented to the Chinese in 1960, and which is to be found on the first page of the *Report of the Officials* to which reference has already been made. The relevant passage reads as follows:

It [the boundary] leaves the main crest of the Kuen Lun mountains at a point approximately Long. 80°21′E and descends in a south-westerly direction, separating the basins of the Amtogor and Sarigh Jilganang lakes in India from those of the Leighten and Tsoggar lakes in Tibet, down to the Lanak Pass.

The point where the Indian-claimed boundary leaves the Kunlun crest is marked on Maps 15 and 19. It will be seen that if indeed the line then proceeds in a southwesterly direction from here, it will cut across some streams flowing into the Amtogor Lake, thus behaving in contradiction to the verbal definition. In this region, it would seem, the Indian definition of the claimed boundary is not entirely clear, since the Indian definition (reinforced by much other Indian argument elsewhere) involves a watershed line.[15] It will be seen from the right hand of Map 7, however, that whichever alignment this Indian claim line may follow, it still will not, on a modern map, bring about a situation in which the 1899 line meets the Indian claim line at a point east of the 80th meridian, unless the principles of the 1899 alignment, as stated in the note, are disregarded. I will comment on the importance of this issue, whether the line ends *east* or *west* of 80°E longitude, a little later on in this paper.

What validity as an Indian boundary can be ascribed to the alignment set out in the British note to the Chinese Foreign

---

[15] The question of watersheds has certainly given rise to a great deal of confusion, compounded by the conflict between the 1899 line and subsequent Indian claims. Map 8, which shows the traces of the Ladakh boundary from three sources, Drew in 1874 (and Drew was basing this line on work done in the service of the Maharaja of Kashmir), the United States Army in 1950, and the United States Air Force in 1947, indicates a wide divergence between possible boundary alignments.

Office (the Tsungli Yamen as this institution was then called) of 14 March 1899? The Chinese never agreed formally to the boundary in question; but, as I have shown in *The China-India Border* (p. 104), the Sinkiang Provincial Government was consulted and agreed informally to the alignment as being a fair and acceptable one. At one time the Indian Government (British) certainly regarded the 1899 lines as being of some considerable force. Writing of the line in 1907, the Indian Foreign Department in its *Note on the History of the Boundary of Kashmir between Ladakh and Kashgaria*[16], stated that:

prior to 1898 no definite boundary was recognized as existing between Ladak and Kashgar, but that since that date we have been consistent (except with reference to the trivial alteration near Shimshal)[17] in recognizing one definite boundary line, which has been described in detail to the Secretary of State [for India in 1898] and once to the Chinese authorities [in 1899 in MacDonald's note]. At the same time, the Chinese have never accepted our proposed boundary, so that we cannot be held to be committed to abide by it. In regard to the Chinese, it will be seen that their ideas as to the boundary are extremely vague, though it is possible that in view of their boundary pillar and notice board,[18] they would make every effort to avoid having it pushed back beyond the Karakoram.

The Indian Government, by 1907, were not too happy about the implications of the 1899 line, which, they felt, would permit Tsarist Russia, should that power ever take over Sinkiang, to come rather closer to the centres of Indian population than might be desirable on political and strategic grounds. Sir Louis Dane, the Indian Foreign Secretary, however, made it clear in a letter to R. T. W. Ritchie, Secretary to the Political Department of the India Office in London, dated 4 July 1907, that even if the Chinese could be excluded from Aksai Chin by a modification of the 1899 note, the best that could be hoped for would be that this tract could be confirmed in the possession of Tibet. Tibet, of course, with an Anglo-Russian settlement on it being then under negotiation, could be expected to serve as a reasonable buffer against Russian infiltration. Referring to a letter from Ritchie of 3 April 1907, Dane wrote that:

[16] Enclosed in Dane to Ritchie, 4 July 1907. See India Office Political External Files, Paper No. 1227 of 1907.
[17] Shimshal is a region on the present Sino-Pakistani border, and it does not relate to the Aksai Chin question.
[18] This refers to the boundary pillar which the Chinese erected on the summit of the Karakoram Pass in 1892, along with a notice board declaring that 'this board is under the sway of . . . the Emperor of China'. This boundary pillar has become rather obscure in the recent literature on the Sino-Indian boundary dispute; and it is generally referred to as having been located at a point '64 miles south of Suget'. Many commentators have failed to notice that 64 miles south of Suget is in fact the summit of the Karakoram Pass. See *Times Literary Supplement*, 2 Jan. 1964, front page article 'Peking and Delhi'.

I mentioned in that letter that the question of the northern boundary of Kashmir . . . was still under consideration, though, for the time being, we had followed the old maps and gazetteers and had shown the boundary as following the Kuenlun Range from the northeastwards of the Gusherbrum Pass.

The object in showing the boundary as far north as possible was to prevent the possibility of the road being improved [by the Russians or some other hostile power] right up to the Karakoram and the length of difficult country to be traversed reduced, as it is on this difficult country that the defence of northern Kashmir depends.

We have since gone into the question and a copy of a note showing the position in regard to this boundary is appended for your information.

In view of what has passed, we are afraid that the boundary must be withdrawn from the Kuenlun Range to the line detailed on paragraph 10 of the attached note,[19] this being the boundary indicated to the Home Government in 1898 and to the Chinese authorities in 1899, and unless there is any objection this will now be done.

We hope, however, to be able to keep Aksai Chin in Tibet in order to adhere to the Kuenlun boundary for that country, as far as possible, and we are having enquiries instituted with a view to determining, if possible, the southernmost marks of Chinese jurisdiction in the neighbourhood of the Kuenlun Range.[20]

Dane makes it clear in this letter that he considers that the 1899 alignment marks the effective British border, even if

[19]Referring to the *Note on the History of the Boundary*, op. cit.
[20]This letter is to be found in India Office Political External Files, Paper No. 1227 of 1907.

that border might be with Tibet rather than with China in this particular region. As the British border, the 1899 line is shown on the Indian Foreign Department map of 1908, prepared specially for the 1909 edition of Aitchison's *Collection of Treaties*, and referred to earlier. The 1899 line is also shown as the British border in the Map of Kashgaria, scale $26\frac{1}{2}$ miles to the inch, prepared by the Intelligence Division of the British Chief of Staff in September 1907 (No. 4, 165 —I., 1907, Intelligence Branch Topo. Dy. No. 5824). There is some considerable evidence, therefore, that at least in the period 1907-8 the 1899 line was regarded in official British circles as the international boundary of British India, a boundary which, again for this limited period, was certainly delimited. After 1907-8 the history of the 1899 line becomes rather obscure, but it is illuminated by a few isolated facts which are worth considering.

In 1912 the Indian Government, fearing that the outbreak of the Chinese Revolution would provide the occasion for the Russian occupation of Sinkiang, once more began to consider where the northern frontier of Kashmir should run. On 12 September 1912 the Viceroy, Lord Hardinge, telegraphed the Secretary of State for India, Lord Crewe, to the effect that a more advanced boundary in this region would now be desirable; and he added that such a boundary should include

'Aksai Chin plain in our territory'.[21] The telegram is not entirely clear in its wording, but the implication seems to be that Aksai Chin was not at that moment formally British, an omission which should be rectified.

Lord Hardinge's proposals were not acted upon. By 1914, still with the objective in mind of keeping the Russians as far away as possible, the Indian Government appears to have hit upon another solution to the Aksai Chin problem, one already indicated by Sir Louis Dane in 1907. During the Simla Conference, when the chief British Delegate, Sir Henry McMahon was busy drawing boundary lines on maps designed to create buffers between Chinese and British territory, a somewhat indirect attempt seems to have been made to obtain Chinese agreement that Aksai Chin was Tibetan rather than Chinese. The map attached to both texts of the Simla Convention, of 27 April 1914 and 3 July 1914, shows in red what are described as 'the frontiers of Tibet'.[22] The right hand, or eastern, extremity of this red line is the now famous 'McMahon Line' defining a boundary between British India and Tibet in the Assam Himalayas. The left hand, or western, extremity of this red line shows the Tibetan boundary in the region of the northern edge of Aksai Chin. The Indian Government of late has maintained that the whole of this red line, shown on a map which the Chinese Delegate to the Simla Conference, Chen I-fan, initialled on 27 April 1914, is a definition of boundaries binding in international law.[23] India, indeed, has placed great emphasis on this particular line as proof that the 'McMahon Line' has been accepted by both China and India. If on these grounds the 'McMahon Line' is a valid boundary, however, then so too, it seems, must be the left hand, or western, extremity of the red line of which the 'McMahon Line' forms part. We must now, therefore, examine this particular piece of the red line, hitherto ignored in the literature.[24]

The western end of the red line on the map attached to both texts of the Simla Convention comes to an abrupt stop at about 79°E longitude. For nearly a degree westwards of 80°E longitude this line follows exactly the same course as the present Indian Government now maintains its boundary with

---

[21] Quoted in *China-India Border*, op. cit., pp. 108-9.
[22] These maps have been published. See India, Ministry of External Affairs, *Atlas of the Northern Frontier of India*, op. cit.; Olaf Caroe, 'The Sino-Indian Question', *Royal Central Asian Journal* L, 3 and 4 (July-Oct. 1963).
[23] See, for example, India, Ministry of External Affairs, *Notes, Memoranda and Letters exchanged between the Governments of India and China, November 1959-March 1960*, White Paper No. III, New Delhi 1960, p. 93.
[24] A slightly simplified tracing of the Simla Convention map is reproduced here as Map 9.

China should follow.[25] This involves a logical absurdity. The Sino-Tibetan boundary cannot possibly, for any of its length, have exactly the same alignment as the Sino-Indian boundary: to suppose otherwise would involve the creation of a four dimensional geography. In 1914, therefore, the British Indian Government must have recognised as being Tibetan some territory touching this particular red line which the Indian Government now claims is Indian. If this is so, then the present Indian Government must, if only tacitly, challenge the validity of this particular line for some of its length at least as a binding boundary definition. If, however, it denies the validity of one part of the line, how can it maintain with such unswerving conviction the validity of another part of the line? There is a problem here, it would seem, which requires some Indian comment.

In view of what we have already seen of British Indian policy towards Aksai Chin as indicated in Dane's letter of 1907, it may perhaps be reasonable to suppose that the alignment of the western end of the red line on the Simla Convention map was intended by the British Delegation, who drew it, to be a device whereby Tibetan control of Aksai Chin would be confirmed, perhaps unawares, by the Chinese. If this line of argument has any merit, then we may assume that in 1914 the Indian Government still did not regard Aksai Chin as falling within its territory, and that it still considered its boundary here as following the 1899 alignment. Then how did India ever acquire a claim to Aksai Chin?

There is evidence to suggest that in 1927 the Indian Government, after a period of considering more advanced boundaries, returned once more to the 1899 alignment.[26] This decision, however, did not then find expression on official Indian maps, which tended on the whole to mark the northern and northeastern boundaries of Kashmir as being 'undefined'. While the 1899 alignment was in general adopted at this time, however, in the Aksai Chin region, it would seem that it was departed from so as to bring this desolate tract, still regarded as a potentially useful buffer between British India and a possible Russian dominated Sinkiang, into British India. Perhaps the Indian Government concluded that no one would notice. After all, the western end of the red line on the Simla Convention maps appeared to have gone unremarked upon by any of the parties concerned. If this argument has any merit, then it would seem that the

---

[25]This situation is shown on Map 10. Map 11 indicates the evolution, in British eyes and those of their Indian successors, of the status of the Aksai Chin area, which moves from being part of Sinkiang to being part of Tibet (the clear implication of the 1914 Simla Convention map), to part of India (the substance of the Indian claim vis-à-vis China).
[26]Lamb, *China-India Border*, op. cit., p. 112.

independent Indian Government inherited, probably unknowingly, this piece of British cartographic annexation undertaken in 1927. All this, it must be emphasised, is no more than informed speculation, since none of the relevant documents of this period have as yet been made public.

Is the 1899 note binding on the Indian Government? As a note, it does not have anything like the force of a treaty. Yet, it contained a clear indication of British intentions, and constituted, as it were, a firm offer to the Chinese Government. Its withdrawal or the modification of its terms, one would think, ought to have been accompanied by some formal intimation to the Chinese Government that the British no longer considered the terms of the 1899 note to represent the British point of view. The published evidence suggests that no such communication was ever made to the Chinese. This cannot possibly mean that the 1899 note is still, as it were, in force. It does mean, however, that the Chinese could still, taking the note at its face value, accept its terms and proceed to occupy Aksai Chin on the grounds that the British, acting on behalf of the then Government of India, had recognised their rights there. The Chinese, during the course of the Sino-Indian boundary dispute, have for some reason best known to themselves never done this, which throws much light on the nature of their diplomatic methods but does not in any way affect the implications, past and present, of the 1899 note.

Why bother about the 1899 line at all? The answer to this question is very simple indeed. As has already been noted, the 1899 line would, if now accepted, place upon the Chinese side all the territory through which runs the Chinese road linking Sinkiang to Western Tibet. Some Indian observers, notably Dr S. Gopal (who, as Director of the Historical Division of the Indian Ministry of External Affairs, was in a position to have informed views on such matters),[27] have declared that the 1899 line, far from giving the Chinese the road, actually cuts across it. This would indeed be true if we accepted the verbal definition of the line in the 1899 note at its face value. If the 1899 line indeed ran to 'a little east of 80° East Longitude', then it would in fact cut the road just at its eastern end. As I have already shown, however, if the 1899 line is plotted on a modern map, following its geographical description, then it would end a little *west* of 80°E longitude, and it would not touch the road at all. This can be seen, perhaps, if the following description of the road, provided by the Indian Government, is applied to Maps 6 and 19:

[27] *Times Literary Supplement*, 6 Feb. 1964, letter from Dr S. Gopal.

the road enters Indian territory just east of Sarigh Jilganang, runs north-west to Amtogar and striking the western bank of the Amtogar lake runs north-west through Yangpa, Khitai Dawan and Haji Langar which are all in indisputable Indian territory. Near the Amtogar lake several branch tracks have also been made motorable.[28]

Indian critics may perhaps object that, even if the 1899 line should have stopped a little west of 80°E longitude, the note does in fact say that it stopped a little east of 80°E longitude: hence, in international law, east of 80°E longitude it is. This is an interesting line of argument which I am qualified neither to follow nor to refute. It is worth noting, however, that the Indian Government itself has, in relation to the McMahon Line, denied validity to this particular reasoning. The Chinese have claimed that just before their attacks in the autumn of 1962 the Indians were in occupation of positions on the Tibetan (hence Chinese) side of the McMahon Line as that line is defined on the original 1914 map. In an annexure to a letter from Mr Nehru to Chou En-lai, dated 14 November 1962, the Indian side refuted this charge by pointing out that too much reliance should not be placed upon the accuracy of the 1914 map on which 'the parallels and meridians were shown only approximately in accordance with the progress achieved at that time in the sphere of scientific surveys'.[29] The McMahon Line, the Indian side declares, follows certain watersheds; and if those watersheds, when determined after examination on the ground, do not coincide precisely with the co-ordinates indicated on the 1914 map, then the watersheds in question, not the map, should be accepted as the valid boundary. We have a very similar situation in the case of the 1899 boundary in Aksai Chin, where the intended watersheds do not entirely agree, when traced on the ground today, with the co-ordinates given on the basis of survey knowledge available at the time when the alignment was defined. If it is absurd, as the Indian side claim, to be bound by archaic cartography in the Assam Himalayas, is it likewise absurd to be so bound in the Karakoram or the Kunlun.

[28] India, Ministry of External Affairs, *Notes, Memoranda and Letters exchanged and Agreements signed between the Governments of India and China 1954-1959*, White Paper, New Delhi 1959, p. 26, Informal Note given by the Indian Foreign Secretary to the Chinese Ambassador, 18 Oct. 1958.

[29] India, Ministry of External Affairs, *Notes, Memoranda and Letters exchanged between the Governments of India and China, October 1962-January 1963*, White Paper No. VIII, New Delhi 1963, pp. 15-16.

# II Aksai Chin and the Raskam crisis: boundary definition in the Karakoram, 1895-1907

## The Strategic Implications of the 1895 Pamirs Settlement

The Pamirs settlement of 1895 marks the end of a series of Anglo-Russian crises over the alignment of the northern frontier of Afghanistan. From the Zulfikar Pass on the Persian border northwest of Herat to Pavalo-Schveikhovski Peak on the watershed between the Little and Taghdumbash Pamirs and the fringes of Chinese jurisdiction, a frontier had been settled beyond major Anglo-Russian dispute. The stretches from the Zulfikar Pass to the Oxus and from Lake Victoria (Sarikol or Wood's Lake) to the Taghdumbash had been carefully laid down on the ground by Anglo-Russian Boundary Commissions in the 1880s and early 1890s, and the presence of boundary pillars gave a promise of permanence and stability which had not hitherto been a feature of Afghan borders. Between these two stretches lay a boundary along the course of the Oxus and the Ab-i-Panja, an alignment which had been more or less settled in principle through Anglo-Russian discussion in London and St Petersburg over the years 1869-73.[1] With demarcated boundaries on both flanks, the

---

[1] The negotiations are discussed in detail by Alder, op. cit., pp. 165-299. There were three sets of discussions involved. Between 1869 and 1873 the British Foreign Secretaries Lord Clarendon and his successor Lord Granville negotiated with the Russians an agreement that the western sector of the northern Afghan frontier should follow the line of the Oxus and its major tributary the Ab-i-Panja.

Oxus line, though it remained subject to minor disputes arising mainly from the tendency of the river to change its course, became secure from major deflections, and it has continued so to the present day.

As a conclusion to the problem of the whereabouts of the northern frontier of Afghanistan, the 1895 settlement was most satisfactory to the British. It served to provide a link by way of the Wakhan salient between the northern Afghan border with Russian territory and the Anglo-Afghan border which had been defined in principle by the Durand Agreement of 1893; and thus the theoretical limits to the northwest of British territory on the Indian subcontinent had been settled in outline. As a barrier against Russia, however, either in the shape of a military advance or the extension of intrigue and what now would be called 'subversion', the 1895 settlement

This agreement was extremely imprecise as, firstly, the full geographical implications of these terms were not at the time understood and, secondly, the river line certainly did not coincide precisely with the territorial ideas entertained by the rulers of Afghanistan. After the Panjdeh crisis of 1885 an Anglo-Russian commission proceeded to demarcate on the ground a boundary line between Afghan and what had now become Russian territory from the Hari Rud at the Zulfikar Pass to a point on the Oxus: this boundary received formal Anglo-Russian sanction in 1887. The final stage, from the source of the Ab-i-Panja in Lake Victoria to the edge of Chinese territory in the Taghdumbash Pamir was defined in 1895. The evolution of boundaries in northern Afghanistan, the Pamirs, and the western Karakoram is illustrated in Maps 12 and 13.

had its defects. When the Pamirs problem began to develop in the early 1890s the Indian Government had hoped that it might be possible to keep the Russians out of much more of the Pamirs than in fact proved to be the case. An attempt was made to bring Roshan and Shignan into Afghanistan and to keep the Alichur and Great and Little Pamirs within China. All this would have resulted in a fairly massive Sino-Afghan buffer between Russian and British territory. Thus, the British supported Chinese and Afghan claims in the region, but their support, without the backing of force, was ineffective against the Russian patrols based on Murghab (Pamirsky Post). By 1895, with the exception of the Pamir-i-Wakhan, which the Amir of Afghanistan was with some difficulty persuaded to accept as part of his dominions, and the Taghdumbash Pamir, which still lay rather insecurely within the Chinese grasp, all the Pamirs had fallen into the Russian sphere.

From the British point of view the most alarming feature of this Russian penetration into the Pamirs was not so much that it had taken place than that it had no obvious limit to its eastward continuation. During the Pamirs negotiations the British had hoped that Chinese participation might be secured; and the Indian Government did its best to bring the Chinese into the boundary demarcation of 1895 with the intention of defining the Russo-Chinese border once the

## II AKSAI CHIN AND THE RASKAM CRISIS: BOUNDARY DEFINITION IN THE KARAKORAM, 1895-1907

Russo-Afghan line had been laid down on the ground. The Pamirs settlement, as it worked out in practice, left a stretch of undefined Russo-Chinese boundary northwards from Pavalo-Schveikhovski Peak to the end of the 1884 Russo-Chinese border east of the Kara Kul lake. Unless plugged, this gap marked the obvious target of further Russian advance; and through it lay the road for the extension of the Tsarist Empire into Chinese Turkestan. Thus the Pamirs settlement of 1895 immediately induced British strategists to consider the role of Chinese Turkestan in future Anglo-Russian relations.

During the Yakub Bey[2] period the British had hoped to create a Kashgarian equivalent of the kind of state that many British officials believed Afghanistan could be, free and independent in internal matters but with its foreign relations under British control. There was certainly no intention in the 1860s and 1870s of a British annexation beyond the ranges of the Karakoram. Without the physical presence there of British forces, could the continued independence of Kashgaria from Russian domination be guaranteed in the 1890s? This question, as the Boundary Commissioners were preparing for their work in the Pamirs, much occupied the attention of George Macartney,[3] who had been living in Kashgar, as Special Assistant for Chinese Affairs to the Resident in Kashmir, for some four years.

Macartney, in a memorandum which he sent off in April 1895, gave it as his opinion that the danger at that moment of a Russian annexation of Kashgaria was greater than it had been in the Yakub Bey period when the Russians had taken over the Ili valley in Dzungaria. The opening of the Trans-Caspian railway had greatly augmented Russian power in Central Asia. This line had by then reached Samarkand, and was soon to be extended to Tashkent and Andijan, the last

[2] Between the late 1860s and 1878 Sinkiang (or Chinese Turkestan as the region was then known to Europeans) was dominated by the Kokandi adventurer Yakub Bey; and it looked for a time as if the region would pass completely out of the Chinese sphere and emerge as either an independent state something like Afghanistan or a régime influenced by either Russia or the British. The story of British policy during this era has been told ably enough by Alder and needs no repetition here. In 1878 the Chinese completed the reconquest of the region, which they named in 1883 or 1884 Sinkiang, The New Dominion. This development changed the strategic situation, but right up to the end of British rule in the Indian subcontinent the question remained whether the Chinese central authorities, Manchu or Republican, could hold Sinkiang in the face of Russian pressure.

[3] George Macartney was the son of Sir Halliday Macartney who, by virtue of his close friendship with a number of important officials in the Manchu hierarchy, exercised great influence over Chinese foreign policy in the 1870s and 1880s and, at times, was effectively Chinese representative in London. The author has been informed, but has been unable to check, that George Macartney's mother was Chinese. If so, the younger Macartney was probably unique among officials at the disposal of the Government of India in his understanding of Chinese ideas and attitudes.

town being but eleven days' march from Kashgar. Should a war break out between Russia and China, Macartney thought, Tsarist forces would immediately occupy all of Dzungaria and the western edge of Kashgaria including the towns of Kashgar and Yarkand. Such an advance was likely in the very near future. The Sino-Japanese war then raging was demonstrating to all who cared to see that Chinese military strength was negligible; and, with Moslem rebellion in full flood in Kansu, nowhere were the Chinese weaker than in Turkestan. It needed only another outbreak of rebellion in Turkestan to provide Russia with an excuse such as she had exploited in 1871 to justify her occupation of Ili on the grounds that she needed to ensure tranquility in regions so close to her borders. This time, Macartney thought, the Russians would not be so rash as to promise to end their occupation once peace was restored. There would be no repetition of the evacuation of Ili. As evidence of possible Russian designs towards Kashgaria, Macartney pointed to the presence on Russian soil of both Bey Kuli Bey, the son of Yakub Bey, and Hakim Khan Torah, a descendant of the Khojas who had ruled Kashgaria in the days before the Manchu conquest in the eighteenth century. Thus the Russians had to hand the leadership for a national anti-Chinese rebellion under Tsarist sponsorship.

In these circumstances, what should British policy be? It was clearly in the interest of the Indian Government to see the Chinese in firm control of Kashgaria. But could the Chinese maintain such control, even with British help? Their officials were corrupt and lazy. Their military were inefficient. The Chinese, as a race, were impervious to outside advice. Even a properly appointed British official in Kashgaria, with all the trappings of the rank of Consul or Political Agent (which Macartney did not then possess) could do little more than watch events and report on them. It was extremely unlikely that he could stiffen Chinese resolve to resist effectively a determined Russian advance. Yet the British could not afford to ignore a Russian penetration into Kashgaria because this would bring the Russian Empire into direct territorial contact with the British all along the Karakoram Range. Hunza, Baltistan, and Ladakh would touch on Russia to their north.

Macartney proposed two courses of action. First, the forthcoming Pamirs Boundary Commission should produce a Sino-Russian as well as a Russo-Afghan border in the Pamirs. This would certainly not prevent a further Russian advance, but at least, by removing uncertainties, it would make that advance a bit more difficult. The real answer, however, lay less in acting through the Chinese than in the British undertaking some measures of their own. The second and essential point, so Macartney thought, was to create some kind of viable buffer along the Karakoram watershed between British territory and a Russian dominated Kashgaria. In other words, could not the British bring about something like the Wakhan tract along their entire northern border from Afghanistan to Tibet? The raw material lay to hand in the rights of the Mir of Hunza in Raskam and the Taghdumbash Pamir and in the claims of the Maharaja of Kashmir to possession of Shahidulla on the middle reaches of the Karakash River.

The question of the Hunza rights north of the main watershed was to develop in the next few years into something like an international crisis, and we shall have cause later on to consider these rights in detail. In 1895 their full nature was still little understood by the British, but Macartney knew that in the days before the establishment of British influence in Hunza the Mir used to collect grazing taxes from the nomads who entered the upper valleys of the Taghdumbash Pamir. His rights appear to have extended from the main watershed northwards to just beyond the point where Karachukur and Uprang Rivers join to form the Tashkurgan River; and he may have possessed claims even further north into Sarikol. In the Raskam region, that is to say in the upper valleys of the Yarkand (or Raskam) River, the Mir, Macartney thought, had territorial claims north of the Shimshal Pass, and he was still in occupation of a place called Darwaza on the road from the Shimshal Pass to the Muztagh River.[4]

To the east of Raskam the claims of Hunza gave way to those of Kashmir. On the Karakash River, for example, Macartney remembered that in 1864 the Maharaja of Kashmir had built a fort and stationed a small garrison at Shahidulla as a measure of protection for caravans on the road between Leh and Yarkand. By 1895 the Shahidulla fort had long been abandoned, and there had been no Kashmiri presence to the north of the Karakoram Pass since the Chinese had overthrown the Kashgarian state of Yakub Bey. The Kashmir Durbar, however, had not forgotten the Shahidulla fort. From time to time it petitioned the Government of India for permission to re-establish its influence beyond the Karakoram Range, but the appeals were uniformly rejected. However, the Kashmir claim, weak though it might be, still persisted.

Macartney then proposed that the claims of Hunza and Kashmir should be put to use. The British should point out their existence to the Chinese, and should propose their being placed on record in an Anglo-Chinese treaty. In this the British should, on behalf of Hunza and Kashmir, waive these claims so long as the area which they affected, and its immediate neighbours, remained under Chinese occupation. If, however, Chinese control could not be maintained, then

[4] See Map 16.

these regions would revert to the British sphere. The Chinese, Macartney thought, while they would be certain to reject the Hunza and Kashmir claims as such, might yet be prepared to see them embodied in a treaty in this form. After all, it could serve only to reinforce Chinese possession of the area. If, however, the Chinese had to go, then the regions covered by the Hunza and Kashmir claims would not fall automatically to Russia but would become, if only in some rather nebulous shape, British. Macartney clearly did not believe that these tracts could be held physically by the British in such circumstances, but he saw no reason why they should not become counters in Anglo-Russian bargaining. The end result, he thought, might possibly be the creation of a 'neutral state' or 'neutral zone' along the crest of the ranges all the way from Afghanistan to Tibet.

Macartney's suggestion was one in outline only, of course. He did not make very clear what would be the nature of sovereignty in this 'neutral zone'. It could hardly remain Chinese if the Russians actually annexed Kashgaria, since it would in these circumstances be in direct contact with no Chinese territory other than, perhaps, Tibet. Possibly Macartney had in mind some kind of artificial state nominally under the sovereignty of Kashmir, which was in theory the suzerain of Hunza, though this would have been less a 'neutral' tract than a British one, and as such would no doubt have to be accepted by Anglo-Russian agreement. Perhaps Macartney envisaged a kind of no man's land, possibly assigned to the sovereignty of some local chieftainship specially created for this purpose, its independence being guaranteed by both the British and the Russians.

Both Lord Elgin's Government of India and the India Office under Lord George Hamilton saw the logic of Macartney's arguments, but, like Macartney, they were not entirely clear in their minds on how to proceed in detail. Major General Gerard, the chief British representative on the Pamirs Boundary Commission, managed to secure from his Russian colleague an assurance that the Taghdumbash Pamir lay within Chinese territory. This, lacking any formal Sino-Russian boundary agreement, was reassuring. It did not, however, allay the fear expressed by Macartney that all Kashgaria would sooner or later fall to Russia. It was certainly possible to overestimate the value of assurances given by subordinate Russian officials and unsupported by any treaty. Lord Elgin, therefore, suggested that the time was opportune for the consideration of some Sino-British agreement on the entire frontier between Hunza and Kashmir on the one hand, and Chinese Turkestan on the other. Perhaps the Chinese might agree that if they were ever obliged to give up the Taghdumbash Pamir it would 'lapse' to Hunza, but, more important, a Sino-Indian boundary should be defined 'whereby a definite limit would be placed to possible extensions of Russian territory towards the Mustagh and Karakoram mountains'. The Chinese, it seemed, could be made to see a boundary agreement of this kind as the British *quid pro quo* for the recent Chinese settlement of her border with French territory across the Mekong.[5]

Perhaps it was a good time to talk about boundaries with the Chinese, but it was pointless for the British to do so until they had obtained a firm impression of where exactly they wanted their frontier to run. In the Karakoram the British had still to evolve definite boundary theories. They had been in possession of detailed knowledge of the region for less than a decade and only since the Pamirs settlement of 1895 had the parameters within which their ideas could develop been laid down with the establishment of a fixed point on the British western flank, namely the Pavalo-Schveikhovski Peak. From the experience of men like Younghusband and Macartney it was clear that there were two basic approaches open to the British. They could either accept a boundary following the main Karakoram watershed, abandoning all that lay to its north, or they could struggle to establish some British footing along a portion at least of the southern rim of the Tarim Basin. Both courses presented their problems. More information was needed for a solution in detail, and more thought and discussion for a solution in principle. Thus Macartney's memorandum of 1895 gave rise to a boundary debate rather than to an immediate boundary settlement; and, as perhaps the present Indian Government may have cause to regret, that debate never did produce the boundary settlement which Macartney thought so desirable, though it nearly achieved it in 1899.

The problem of the British border with Kashgaria which Macartney had raised aroused the interest of Sir John Ardagh, Major General and Director of Military Intelligence. Ardagh had served in India on the staff of the Viceroy, Lord Lans-

[5]For Macartney's memorandum, dated 16 April 1895, and for its discussion by the Government of India under Lord Elgin, see FO 17/1255, Elgin to Hamilton No. 186 of 25 Sept. 1895 enclosed in India Office to Foreign Office 18 Oct. 1895. The *quid pro quo* would be based on the following circumstances. In 1894, in an attempt to create some kind of buffer along the Mekong River between the limits of British influence in the Burmese Shan States and the expanding French power in Laos, the British had accepted Chinese sovereignty over a portion of one of the major Shan States, Kengtung. The bulk of Kengtung lay on the western side of the Mekong but one tract, Kiang Hung, claimed by Kengtung, lay on the eastern side of the river. The British acknowledged Chinese rights here on the condition that China did not cede Kiang Hung to any other power. In 1895 China in fact violated this undertaking by ceding some of the territory involved to France. In the event the British did not exploit this situation vis-à-vis the Chinese in the Pamirs and the Karakoram, but in 1897 they used it as their justification for ending once and for all the remaining symbols of Burmese status as a Chinese tributary and for a number of adjustments along the Sino-Burmese border. See Lamb, *Asian Frontiers*, op. cit., p. 154.

downe, when he had compiled a number of memoranda on the problem of Indian defence. He had from the outset been an advocate of a 'forward' policy, that is to say a policy which aimed at keeping the Russian enemy as far away as possible from the centres of Indian population, even if this also involved a territorial expansion of British India beyond the limits dictated by considerations of administrative simplicity. His close observation of the progress of the Pamirs crisis had served only to reinforce his conclusions. It should cause no surprise, therefore, that Ardagh evolved a boundary policy of a rather more positive nature than that indicated in Macartney's memorandum of April 1895. This policy was contained in a document entitled 'The Northern Frontier of India—from the Pamirs to Tibet', which Ardagh despatched to the Foreign Office and the India Office on New Year's Day, 1897. Ardagh's memorandum enjoyed considerable influence. It continued to be discussed right up to the end of British rule in the Indian subcontinent. There are grounds for believing that it still influences Indian strategists today. Its implications found their way onto a number of British maps. That its suggestions did not, in fact, become established British policy does not detract from its significance; and we shall have to consider it in some detail here.

Ardagh's basic assumption, which had also been that of Macartney, was that 'the collapse of China in the late China-Japan war showed the futility of our trusting to that power as a possible ally, and there is every reason to believe that she will be equally useless as a buffer between Russia and the Northern Frontier of India'. To the war with Japan must be added the effects of the Moslem rebellion in Kansu which weakened seriously the Chinese hold over a district straddling the main Chinese line of communication between Peking and Kashgar. Finally, Ardagh noted, Macartney had been reporting riots and plots in Kashgaria itself, where the Chinese military appeared to be on the verge of mutiny. All this, Ardagh thought 'probable', was the overture to a Russian occupation of Kashgaria, a region far richer and more fertile than the Pamir tracts which Russia had not hesitated to annex in the early 1890s. When would the Russians move towards Kashgar? Not at once, Ardagh thought, but surely within his lifetime, and 'if the eventual annexation of Kashgaria by Russia is to be expected, we may be sure that Russia, as in the past, will endeavour to push her boundary as far south as she can, for political reasons, even if no real military advantage is sought'. Hence, he concluded, 'it is evident that sooner or later we shall have to conclude a definite agreement regarding the northern frontier of India'.

Where should that frontier be? Hitherto British strategists had looked on the great mountain ranges to the north of Chitral, Hunza, and Ladakh as 'the natural frontier of India'.

## II AKSAI CHIN AND THE RASKAM CRISIS: BOUNDARY DEFINITION IN THE KARAKORAM, 1895-1907

These mountains had much to recommend them. They marked a limit to British rule easy to define; they were, on the whole, difficult to cross; and they formed a reasonable ethnic divide. However, as a frontier to be defended, these mountains posed their problems. One could hardly establish a line of defence along the actual watershed, which passed through some of the highest and most difficult terrain in the world. The prospect of permanent border posts on the Kilik, Mintaka, and Karakoram Passes, let alone even more formidable passes like the Muztagh, was impossible to contemplate. The British in the 1890s could no more hope to hold a line based on such passes than could the Indian Republic hold, as it found to its cost in 1962, as a defensive position, the Se La Pass in the Assam Himalayas. The key to the defence of a mountain line of this kind was the possession of adequate intelligence as to what was going on beyond it. It was essential to know what was happening on the other side of the hill.

The northern frontier, from the Pamirs to Tibet, could be approached by an enemy, by which term Sir John Ardagh understood the Russians and no one else, from four main directions. Firstly, from the newly acquired territory in the Pamirs the Russians could cross the Beyik Pass into the Taghdumbash Pamir and thence strike at the passes leading southwards from the valleys of the Karachukur and Uprang Rivers. Secondly, these same passes could also be approached from a Kashgarian base by a route up the Tashkurgan River from its junction with the Yarkand River. Thirdly, a Russian force in Kashgaria could advance up the Yarkand River and either attack Hunza territory across the Shimshal Pass by way of the Muztagh River, or continue up the Yarkand (or Raskam) River to the Karakoram Pass and the way into Ladakh. Finally, from the valleys of the Karakash River there were possible, though certainly difficult, routes into Ladakh across the Aksai Chin plateau. The Yarkand and its tributaries and the Karakash thus offered approaches to the mountain barrier over a wide front; and Ardagh thought that the correct strategy, in this particular environment, was to establish some measure of British control over the upper reaches of the valleys of these rivers flowing into the Tarim basin.

The British border, Ardagh therefore argued, should follow not the line of the Karakoram watershed but rather the crests, insofar as it could be arranged, of a series of ranges to the north of the Karakoram, ranges through which passed the upper courses of the Yarkand and Karakash systems. Starting in the west at the Beyik Pass or at Pavalo-Schveikhovski Peak, the line which Ardagh favoured would not run southwards around the head of the Karachukur Valley along the Karakoram watershed: rather, it would run due east to cross the Tashkurgan River just to the north of the junction of its Karachukur and Uprang tributaries near a point marked on the maps of the time as Dehda or Kurghan-i-Ujadbai (Younghusband's name). Across the Tashkurgan River the line would continue eastwards across the crest of the Muztagh Ata Range and then, still running more or less due east, across the Yarkand River and up to the crest of the Kunlun Range. The Yarkand would be crossed at a point about 50 miles north of the junction with its Muztagh tributary. Once on the crest of the Kunlun, Ardagh's suggested line ran southeastwards along the watershed between the Yarkand (or Raskam) and the Karakash until it reached the Yangi Pass, where it turned slightly northeastwards along what is sometimes known as the Kilian Range. Running then along this range, which marked the watershed on the northern side of the Karakash as it executed its great bend towards the Taklamakan desert, the line crossed the Sanju (or Grim) Pass and continued eastwards until just after the 79th meridian of east longitude, when it turned sharply southeastwards to cross the Karakash and climb up to the Kunlun crest, which it reached at the second Yangi Pass. From here onwards it followed more or less what the Indians now claim their Aksai Chin border to be.

Ardagh's line, as suggested in his memorandum of 1 January 1897, ran a long way north of the boundary which either India or Pakistan claim today, or which the British were to consider in 1898-99.[6] It was, in fact, at its eastern end almost precisely the same boundary which Johnson thought in 1865 to mark the northern limits of the Kashmir State, and for some of its length it depended upon the same kind of argument that gave rise to Johnson's border. As far as the western part of this line was concerned, it was based on the assumption that the Mir of Hunza's claims to rights in the Taghdumbash Pamir and Raskam, to which Macartney had already drawn attention in 1895, constituted, or could be argued to constitute, British sovereignty. This was probably not an issue of which Johnson was aware. For the eastern portion of his line, however, Ardagh, like Johnson before him, was exploiting the claims of Kashmir to Shahidulla at the apex of the great bend in the Karakash.

By 1897, it must be admitted, the Kashmiri claim to Shahidulla had worn rather thin.[7] The Shahidulla fort, constructed in 1864, had been abandoned by the Kashmiris in 1867 or 1868, and it had not been re-occupied by them since.

[6] For Ardagh's proposed alignment, see Maps 13, 14, and 15.
[7] PSF 1912/82, No. 1227/1907, 'Note on the History of the Boundary of Kashmir between Ladak and Kashgaria', Indian Foreign Department, enclosed in Dane to Ritchie 4 July 1907. This document is a most important summary of the whole question of boundaries in the neighbourhood of the Karakoram Pass. It was drawn up by the Indian Foreign Department in 1907 in reply to a request from the India Office for detailed information on the correct alignment of the British Indian border.

## II AKSAI CHIN AND THE RASKAM CRISIS: BOUNDARY DEFINITION IN THE KARAKORAM, 1895-1907

In 1888 the Kashmiri Durbar had sought to return to Shahidulla, but had been refused permission to do so by the Government of India. On that occasion Sir Mortimer Durand, the Indian Foreign Secretary, applying a line of reasoning diametrically opposed to that which would subsequently be advanced by Sir John Ardagh, remarked that 'it would not be desirable to run the risk of troublesome controversy with China in order to push a Kashmir post beyond the Karakoram with the object of forestalling Russia when she succeeds the Chinese in Yarkand'. By 1890 the Chinese had established themselves in force at Shahidulla and in 1892 they erected a boundary pillar just on the Ladakh side of the summit of the Karakoram Pass. At the same time they began, at their post on the road between Suget Karaul on the Karakash and the Suget Pass (which route led to Ladakh via the Karakoram Pass), to keep a careful check on travellers bound to and from British territory. Thus it was clear that the eastern portion of Ardagh's suggested line embraced territory under undoubted Chinese occupation, and which the Chinese were unlikely to relinquish without much argument, if they could be so persuaded at all. In this respect Ardagh's line was far less viable than such an alignment of the British border would have been in Johnson's day, when Chinese power in Turkestan had collapsed and before Yakub Bey had established himself securely in China's place.

Ardagh certainly appreciated this objection to the eastern sector of his proposed alignment and he offered a substitute for it. From the first, or eastern, Yangi Pass the boundary could run southeastwards along the Suget Range, through the Suget Pass, and then across the Karakash valley near Haji Langar to meet the present Indian claimed border. The result would be to leave Shahidulla on the Chinese side. This alignment is one which is still frequently shown on modern maps, and it has dominated most British maps of this region in the twentieth century.

Once the boundary alignment had been decided upon, Ardagh continued, then further action should be considered. Perhaps, as Macartney had already suggested, the territory between the Karakoram watershed and Ardagh's line might merely be protected by a Chinese agreement that if it were alienated it could only be to the British. Perhaps the tracts in question might be ceded outright by China to the British. Or perhaps, if the moment did not seem opportune for boundary discussions with the Chinese, the British might content themselves with a series of private arrangements with the local chiefs in the tracts concerned designed to establish British supremacy and protection which could be reinforced by the occasional British performance of acts of sovereignty such as the collection of token tax or tribute.[8]

The historical justification for the line proposed by Sir John Ardagh, even in its more moderate form, was nowhere impressively strong, but it was certainly stronger in the west than in the east. A case of sorts could be built up on the claims of the Mir of Hunza over Raskam and the Taghdumbash Pamir, and the latter region was very much on the British side of any eastward extension of the line laid down in 1895 as the Russo-Afghan border in the Pamirs. A further extension could result in the inclusion in the British sphere of Raskam. Once, however, the line reached a point sufficiently far to the east to involve the status of Suget or Shahidulla, then the lack of a convincing legal basis became all too apparent. It was true that the Maharaja of Kashmir had for a few years in the 1860s, when Chinese rule in Kashgaria had collapsed, occupied Shahidulla; but he had long ceased to do so by January 1897. The Government of India had on more than one occasion discouraged Kashmiri plans to re-establish influence to the north of the Karakoram Pass. By the time of the Pamirs Boundary Commission the Chinese authorities in Kashgar had made it quite clear that they considered Chinese territory to extend to the boundary pillar which they had erected on the summit of that Pass. To support a Kashmiri claim to Shahidulla at this late stage would be to challenge a declared Chinese sovereignty to which some significant administrative effect had already been given.

A major defect of the eastern end of Ardagh's line, though this was probably not appreciated by its author, was that it lacked any equivalent to Pavalo-Schveikhovski Peak, any place where it could link up with an already settled boundary. The Ardagh boundary ended in the Kunlun Range to the east of the Yangi Pass where it met the northernmost sector of the eastern boundary of Ladakh as it had been drawn ever since Johnson, in 1865, first introduced the Aksai Chin plateau to British cartography. The Ladakh border had been shown by Johnson as reaching the Kunlun crest by way of the watersheds along the eastern edge of the Sarigh Jilganang and Amtogor basins. No grounds had ever been produced by the Indian Government for this alignment other than those of convenience; and other alignments had been proposed since Johnson's day. The main advantage of the Aksai Chin boundary which Johnson had shown was precisely that it made a boundary such as Ardagh's possible. Only by including some of the Aksai Chin plateau in British territory was it possible to devise a practicable line which was to run along the Kilian Range north of Shahidulla. Had the Kara-

---

[8]Sir John Ardagh's memorandum, 'The Northern Frontier of India —from the Pamirs to Tibet', is to be found in FO 17/1328, Military Intelligence to Foreign Office, 1 January 1897. The text has been printed in Woodman, op. cit., pp. 360-3.

koram Pass and the watershed between the Karakash and the Shyok and its tributaries been accepted, as it had been for example by Trelawney Saunders, Cartographer to the India Office, in 1873 as the British border in the extreme northeast of Ladakh,[9] then the inclusion of Shahidulla would have involved a peculiar eastward pointing salient of British territory north of the Karakoram Range which, apart from its utter indefensibility on military and strategic grounds, would have looked absurd on maps and would, thereby, have invited question by other powers. One advantage of a line of the type Ardagh proposed, with its eastern terminus on the Kunlun Range somewhere in the region of the 80th meridian of east longitude, was that it appeared plausible on maps, giving this corner of British India a nicely squared off look. Such a look the present Indian Government, which has brought back its boundary to the Karakoram Pass while retaining Ardagh's eastern terminus in the Kunlun, has now to some degree abandoned and it should cause no surprise that many modern cartographers are still wedded to the aesthetic features of the moderate variant of Ardagh's line.

Politically, Ardagh's eastern terminus would have been quite satisfactory had it been located in territory in which no other power was interested. Ardagh himself may well have supposed that the desolation of the Aksai Chin plateau and

[9]See Map 15 for the Saunders boundary alignment.

the Kunlun fell into this category, and it may have surprised him to be told that the Chinese had also developed ideas about the ownership of this particular region. To such ideas, however, the Chinese had already given some expression when Sir John Ardagh's memorandum was being drafted, and they were soon to contribute to the evolution of a British boundary proposal rather different from that advanced by the Director of Military Intelligence.

**Chinese Thoughts on a Karakoram Boundary**
In the years immediately following the reconquest of Turkestan (or Sinkiang, the New Dominion, as the region was renamed in 1883 or 1884), the Chinese were too concerned with administrative consolidation and reform and with the problem of getting the Russians out of the Ili to pay much attention to the question of their precise territorial limits in the Pamirs and the Karakoram. In 1881 the Ili boundary was settled by the Treaty of St Petersburg, and in 1884 the rest of the then Sino-Russian border in Sinkiang was defined.[10] This last line terminated in the northeastern Pamirs at the Uzbel Pass a few miles southeast of the Karakul Lake. Below this point the Russians had yet to penetrate in force into the Pamirs. Moreover, at this time (1884) the British had not

[10]For some account of the Sino-Russian Frontier Delimitation Protocol of 22 May 1884, see Alder, op. cit., pp. 242-3.

begun to approach the Pamirs through Hunza and Chitral. The only point of Anglo-Chinese contact was then in the neighbourhood of the Karakoram Pass and there can be no doubt that the Kashgar authorities in 1884 already looked on the Karakoram Pass as a point on their southern boundary, just as they had been accustomed to consider it in the days before Yakub Bey. With the end of Yakub Bey the British, too, tended to accept the Karakoram Pass as the limit of their territory. They consistently refused the Kashmir Durbar permission to cross the pass and re-establish a garrison at Shahidulla.

By the end of the 1880s, with the exploits of Younghusband and Grombtchevski giving clear signs of a growing Anglo-Russian interest in the Pamirs and the Karakoram, the Chinese appreciated that these remote southeastern tracts of Sinkiang could no longer be ignored.[11] From that period the Kashgar authorities began to undertake, with British encouragement, measures to establish their sovereignty as far westwards into the Pamirs as they could; and a number of Chinese posts were established across the Sarikol Range. They also began to show an active interest in the Karakoram border, which

grew in step with the increased tempo of British activity on the other side. Thus it was that the Chinese countered the establishment of British influence in Hunza with a diplomatic struggle to maintain the signs and symbols of their sovereignty over the Mir, a struggle in which, it must be admitted, they emerged for the time being victorious. At the same time the Kashgar authorities began to be more active along the Leh-Yarkand trade route.

It was along this route, the main artery of trade between Chinese Turkestan and the Indian subcontinent, that the two Forsyth Embassies had come in the days of Yakub Bey. It was along this route, moreover, that the Kashmir Durbar had endeavoured, with the Shahidulla fort and garrison, to extend its influence across the mountains to its north. In Kashgar this route must have appeared to provide one of the weakest spots in the Chinese defences. It was also the direction in which Chinese counter-measures could be most easily taken. All that was required was the establishment of an effective check on travellers entering Sinkiang from the south. By 1890 the Chinese had set up a frontier post at Shahidulla, where such a post had been established earlier by Yakub Bey. Another post at Suget, a little further to the south, was, Younghusband reported,

---

[11] The adventures of Francis Younghusband and his rival in Russian employ, the Polish nobleman Captain B. Grombtchevski (or Gromchevsky) are related by Younghusband himself in *The Heart of a Continent*, London 1896, and in Alder, op. cit., and Woodman, op. cit.

then under construction.¹² In that year the Chinese set up a boundary pillar on the summit of the Karakoram Pass.¹³

By 1890 there could be no doubt as to where the Chinese thought their southern border ran. As Chinese officials told Younghusband in that year, and Macartney on subsequent occasions, their boundary followed the Karakoram Range and the watershed between the Indus and the Tarim basin.¹⁴ North of that watershed was Chinese territory, and the northern slopes of the Karakoram were part of the Chinese administrative districts of Yarkand and Khotan. Thus the British, or their Indian subjects, could have no possible claim to places like Shahidulla and Suget, which were in undoubted Chinese territory. The Government of India at that time appears to have agreed. When, in 1892, the Kashmir Durbar once more sought permission to spread north into Suget and Shahidulla, the Kashmir State Council was informed by the British Resident that 'both Shahidulla and Suget were situated in a district inhabited by Khirgiz who had for many years paid tribute to China'. The Resident added that the water which flowed into Yarkand territory was Chinese, in other words, that Kashmir territory ended at the Indus-Tarim watershed.¹⁵ This conclusion was emphasised by pointing to the Chinese boundary pillar on the Karakoram Pass—it is not clear whether this was the same pillar erected in 1890 or a new one. The pillar, which was located some 50 feet from the summit of the Pass on the Ladakh side, bore a notice declaring that 'this board is under the sway of the Emperor of China'.¹⁶ From this period to the present day the Karakoram Pass has continued without interruption to mark the effective Sino-Indian border. By Asian standards it is as well established a boundary point as one can hope to find.

How did the Chinese interpret the alignment of their frontier on either side of the Karakoram Pass? To the west they appear to have considered the line as running along the crest of the Karakoram range, which here is extremely wide, a complex tangle of some of the world's highest peaks and largest glaciers, until Hunza territory was reached. At Hunza the Chinese line, in the sense that Hunza was considered a

---

¹²By 1892, when Lord Dunmore was in Kashgaria, the Suget post was fully operational. There was a notice board outside the post which announced that 'anyone crossing the Chinese Frontier without reporting himself at the fort will be imprisoned'. Suget was the obvious place, at the foot of the Suget Pass leading to the Karakoram Pass, to control the trade from Ladakh across the Karakoram Pass and also by any of the Aksai Chin routes.

¹³FO 539/51, Nos. 1, 3, and 4.
¹⁴FO 539/51, No. 3, enclosing interview between Younghusband and Pau, Amban of Yarkand, 5 Sept. 1890. See also FO 65/1484, India Office to Foreign Office, 15 January 1894 enclosing Macartney, 28 September 1893.
¹⁵PSF 1912/82, No. 1227/1907.
¹⁶Loc. cit.

Chinese tributary, could have been described as turning well south of the main watershed. Before the Sino-Pakistani agreement of 1963, the Chinese Communists showed it thus on their maps. In fact, however, the Chinese never claimed to have exercised direct administration in Hunza, and always admitted the existence of a boundary of some kind between Hunza territory and Chinese Turkestan. This boundary ran in places a little bit to the north of the watershed, though its precise course was subject to some argument. By 1892 it seems that there was no actual Chinese administration in Raskam, and in the Taghdumbash Pamir the last Chinese post, Lord Dunmore reported in 1892, was just north of the junction of the Karachukur and Uprang Rivers.[17] Thus at this period it could have been argued that the Hunza-Sinkiang border followed a line very close to that which Ardagh was to propose for this district in January 1897. By 1897, however, the Chinese had already begun to take steps to challenge any such conclusion and it soon became clear that, with one or two possible minor exceptions, they regarded as the main watershed line the Hunza-Sinkiang border.

What about the territory to the east of the Karakoram Pass? Here a tangle of mountains leads on to the great plateaus of Aksai Chin and Lingzitang, and here the watershed lines of the Kunlun and Karakoram Ranges merge in a complex series of internal drainage basins with outlets neither to the Indus nor to the Tarim basin. Where did the Chinese imagine their frontier to run here? There can be no doubt, as Macartney reported on a number of occasions, that the Chinese felt that some kind of watershed principle should apply here as elsewhere along the Karakoram, and that there could be no question that the entire basin of the Karakash was anything but Chinese. The Karakash valley had from time immemorial been a source of jade, for which the Khotan district was famous, and Chinese subjects had made their way up the river in quest of this stone so esteemed in the Chinese civilised world. The Karakash was also a trade route of sorts and a link between Chinese Turkestan and Tibet. The Dzungars had crossed it in 1717 during their great raid on Lhasa. British missions had come along it in the Forsyth era in the 1870s. No doubt it was one of the channels whereby Chinese manufactured goods, knives, bells, swords, and so on, reached, in western Tibet, population centres like Rudok.

This region is still one of the most desolate on the face of the earth. The British became aware of the rudiments of its topography only in 1865, when Johnson crossed it on his way to Khotan, and it could never have supported anything but a transient population. There certainly could have been no administration here. Any Chinese posts concerned with the

---

[17]Earl of Dunmore, *Report on the Pamirs and Part of Russian Central Asia*, Calcutta 1893.

area would have been located on the lower reaches of rivers flowing into the Tarim basin, just as British posts with a similar interest would have been located in the general neighbourhood of Leh. In these circumstances, then, did the Chinese possess even a vague idea of what the terms Aksai Chin and Lingzitang implied? Were they anything like so well informed about the region as were the British following the explorations of the Forsyth missions? To the second question the answer was certainly negative. Chinese officials have never felt anything like the fascination of their British colleagues for survey, nor did the traditional civilisation of China match nineteenth century western technology in cartographic techniques. The Chinese authorities in Kashgar in the 1890s did, however, concern themselves with the topography of the land to the east of the Karakoram Pass. At the same time as they decided to reassert that Pass as their boundary point, they also, it appears, undertook a survey of the whole Karakoram border region, while a similar survey, in the charge of one Hai Yin, was carried out in the Pamirs.[18]

The Karakoram survey was entrusted to Li Yuan-ping. During 1891 and 1892 he travelled along much of the northern slopes of the Karakoram, and the results of his work, including an incredibly crude map, scarcely intelligible, came to Macartney's notice in 1893. Macartney, however, had no doubt that Li had been, among other places, to the Aksai Chin and Lingzitang tracts, and that here as elsewhere he had reported on a watershed boundary.[19] The precise nature of that boundary to the east of the Karakoram Pass was to become clearer, as we shall see, in 1896. Li's report on this region was produced by the Chinese side in the Sino-Indian discussions of 1960-61, and it is printed in the *Officials' Report*.[20] There is no reason to doubt its authenticity, since it agrees with what Macartney reported. It makes it clear that Li ascended the Karakash to Haji Langar and then crossed Aksai Chin and Lingzitang to the north bank of the Changchenmo River. This was an extremely difficult journey, one to compare with Johnson's traverse in 1865, with the added feat in Li's case of a double crossing of the plateaus without the intervening rest that Johnson enjoyed in some oasis like Khotan. Li's survey, at all events, is evidence that the Kashgar authorities by the middle 1890s had acquired some information on the topography of Aksai Chin and Lingzitang, and it helps explain how they were able, in 1896, to raise specific claims to the Chinese possession of Aksai Chin.

---

[18] FO 65/1485, Memorandum of Information regarding affairs beyond the North-Western Frontier (N.W. Frontier Memo) for Feb. 1894.

[19] FO 65/1484, N. W. Frontier Memo for November & December 1893; India Office to Foreign Office, 15 Jan. 1894.
[20] *Officials' Report*, op. cit., Chinese Report, pp. 80-1.

In July 1893 Macartney reported a piece of evidence which conflicted with the impression of a Chinese belief in a Karakoram watershed boundary which he had derived from other sources.[21] This was the so called 'Hung Tajen's map' which has figured on a number of subsequent occasions in discussions over the correct alignment of the Karakoram boundary. The map in question came to Macartney's notice in Kashgar, and he sent a tracing of it back to the Government of India as a map

> showing the boundary between Chinese and British Kashmir territories; and, at the same time, to draw your attention to the fact that in this map this boundary is not shown as running along the crest of the Karakoram range as one might have supposed if the watershed between the Indus and Yarkand river valleys was to be taken as the boundary; but is shown somewhat to the north of that watershed, and following the banks of that portion of the Yarkand river which was explored by Captain Younghusband in 1889.

Macartney was intrigued by the implications of this map, which he felt might perhaps be exploited by the British at some future date. As he put it:

> whether there would be any advantage in extending our frontier to the northern side of the Karakoram range is a question on which I am incompetent to express an opinion. But it has occurred to me that one day, when the Russians shall have taken possession of Sarikul and Raskam, we may have to consider the advisability, from a strategical point of view, of either advancing or waiving the claims which Kanjut [Hunza] is said to have over certain places beyond its generally recognised boundary; and when such a contingency arises, we may find it to our interest to have all the evidence we can discover to show that the Chinese frontier never actually extended as far as the Karakoram range; and possibly this map of Hung Ta-chen may not be without its use.

What was this map, and who was Hung Tajen? The map is a sheet, one of a series of thirty-five, Macartney reported, of maps relating to the Sino-Russian border region. Macartney, earlier in 1893, had had occasion to report on another sheet in the series which dealt with the Sino-Russian frontier in the Pamirs. He did not state where he got the map, but he did note that the whole series of thirty-five sheets was on public sale in Shanghai, a fact which rather suggests that this was, contrary to the argument raised by the Indian side in the recent Sino-Indian debate, something rather different from an ordinary official Chinese document. Hung Tajen, as Macartney reported, had recently been Chinese Minister in St Petersburg. His full name was Hung Chün. In 1887 he was appointed Chinese Minister to Russia, Germany, Austria, and Holland, a post which he held until 1890 when he returned to Peking to serve as senior vice-president on the

---

[21] Macartney to Barr, Officiating Resident in Kashmir, 23 July 1893.

Board of War and, at the same time, to a post in the Tsungli Yamen, the Chinese Ministry of Foreign Affairs. He died in 1893. During his stay in Europe Hung Chün occupied himself with translating into Chinese a series of Russian maps on the Sino-Russian borderlands. The complete work, thirty-five maps in all, was published in 1890 under the title *Chung Ê chiao-chieh t'u*. It was from this work that Macartney's map originated, though in the tracing which he sent back to the Government Macartney transliterated into Roman script Hung Chün's Chinese characters representing the place names on the original Russian maps.[22] By no stretch of the imagination can Hung Chün's maps be interpreted as official Chinese maps, though it might perhaps be argued that they were official Russian maps in a Chinese version. The full nature of these maps was not, perhaps, understood by Macartney, whose account suggests that they were drawn by Hung Chün himself while in St Petersburg and that they represented an official Chinese opinion. In fact, it does seem that Hung Chün was an advocate of an extremely moderate Chinese policy in Central Asia so as not to arouse the antagonism of the Russians and the British, but this was his own view, not necessarily that of his Government. There can be no question, at all events, that the boundary on Hung Chün's map coincided with the ideas held in 1893 by the Chinese authorities in Kashgar with immediate responsibility for the Karakoram border.

Hung Chün's boundary followed a somewhat more moderate course than that proposed by Ardagh, even in the less advanced alternative. From just north of Haji Langar in the Aksai Chin area it crossed the Karakash in a northwesterly direction to ascend the Suget Range. It then followed that range until the Suget Pass, at which point it turned southwest to meet the Yarkand (or Raskam) River just south of Khapalung. It then followed the Yarkand River downstream to what appears to be its junction with the Muztagh River, which it followed up to the main Karakoram crest. Westwards of this point the Karakoram crest was the boundary. This boundary was a variant of the kind shown on many British maps in the 1870s and 1880s; indeed ever since Johnson's journey to Khotan of 1865 and the publication by the Survey of India of the *Kashmir Atlas* in 1868. No doubt it was copied from some British source by Russian cartographers, and thus passed into Hung Chün's translation.

In 1896, some three years after Macartney had communicated Hung Chün's map to the Government of India, the Kashgar authorities, no doubt in part on the basis of the information provided by Li Yuan-ping, indicated the exist-

---

[22] A.W. Hummel (ed.), *Eminent Chinese of the Ch'ing Period, 1644-1912*, Vol. I, Washington D.C., 1943, pp. 360-1.

ence of a Chinese claim to Aksai Chin.[23] The question arose as the result of Macartney's presentation to the *Taotai*, or Governor, of Kashgar with a copy of W. and A. K. Johnston's *Atlas of India*, 1894 edition, which indicated in the Aksai Chin region a British boundary of the kind first drawn by Johnson (no kin to the publishers of the *Atlas*) in 1865, a boundary also indicated, incidentally, on Hung Chün's map. The *Taotai* evidently showed the *Atlas* to members of the Russian Consulate in Kashgar, who pointed out to the Chinese official that in it the British had marked as theirs much Chinese territory in the Aksai Chin area. The *Taotai* raised this point with Macartney in October 1896, apparently on instructions from the Provincial Governor of Sinkiang in Urumchi. Macartney was inclined, so he reported to the Government of India, to agree with the *Taotai* that the British maps had incorrectly shown the boundary in Aksai Chin, a 'very elevated table-land at the northeast of Ladak, and it was probably the case that part was in Chinese and part in British territory'. The North-West Frontier Intelligence Report of December 1896 notes that Macartney's supposition was correct, indicating that some officials at least in the Indian Foreign Department accepted a partition of the Aksai Chin and Lingzitang plateaus into Chinese and British zones.

At the moment when Sir John Ardagh put his boundary ideas on paper, therefore, the Indian Government had acquired a good picture of the kind of boundary the Chinese considered to be theirs on either side of the Karakoram Pass region; and it was obvious that here the concepts of Ardagh and the Chinese conflicted. By the end of 1896 it was, perhaps, not quite so clear where the Chinese considered their boundary to be along the western part of the Karakoram, and it could still be argued in India that, on the basis of Chinese administrative practice so far demonstrated, a case acceptable in Kashgar could be made for retaining some of Raskam and the Taghdumbash Pamir within the British sphere. The weaknesses in this particular argument, however, began to become apparent in 1897. The development of the Raskam crisis, the subject of the next section, indicated that no more in the west than in the east were the Chinese eager to accept British influence across the Indus-Tarim watershed in the Karakoram.

### The Raskam Crisis: first phase

Mention has already been made of the rights which the Mir of Hunza claimed in Raskam and in the Taghdumbash Pamir.

---

[23] FO 65/1547, N.W. Frontier Memo for Dec. 1896; FO 17/1356, Elgin to Hamilton, 23 Dec. 1897 in India Office to Foreign Office, 22 Jan. 1898.

The precise nature of these rights now needs to be defined.[24] In the Taghdumbash Pamir, which in this context meant, in effect, the valleys of the Karachukur and Uprang Rivers, the Mir felt that he was entitled to the yield of a tax raised on the Kirghiz nomads who grazed their flocks there. This income had been granted to him, the Mir declared, by the Chinese at some period in the eighteenth century, and it had originally included as well the yield of taxes imposed on the Sarikoli inhabitants of the Tashkurgan region further north, though the Sarikolis had ceased payment from about 1885. Originally Hunza agents had collected the tax, and Chinese tax gatherers had been strangers to the southern Taghdumbash. In 1896, however, no doubt as part of the general Chinese policy of making good the Karakoram watershed boundary, the taxes on the Kirghiz started being collected by the Chinese, who then handed them over to the Mir. The Kirghiz had on many occasions appealed to the Chinese authorities to remit these taxes, but the Chinese had always turned a deaf ear. By 1896, therefore, the Mir enjoyed revenue rights in the Taghdumbash Pamir, but it could hardly be maintained that he still exercised sovereignty over the area. The actual revenue collection, which was the sole administration carried out there, was in the hands of the Chinese officer at Tashkurgan, often referred to as the *Amban*. The Mir, and his British suzerains on his behalf, could protest against any loss of revenue. They would find it difficult, however, to maintain that the Taghdumbash Pamir constituted British territory. In the event, as we shall see, British claims to the Taghdumbash Pamir had been tacitly abandoned by 1905.

In Raskam the Hunza rights were more complex. There was reason to believe that Hunza subjects had occupied tracts on the Raskam (or Yarkand), Muztagh, and Uprang Jilga Rivers before the Yakub Bey era. There had been Hunza forts at Azgar and one or two other places on the Yarkand River which had served as bases for Hunza raids on the caravan trade in southern Kashgaria. The Mir had refused requests by others, the Mirs of Wakhan for example, for rights to settle in this region. At this period the Hunza economic interest in Raskam was more piratical than agricultural, but a few plots were cultivated by Hunza people. With the coming of Yakub Bey the Hunza control over Raskam appears to have lapsed, and attempts to revive it were started only after the British occupation of Hunza and Nagar in 1892. This

---

[24]FO 17/1362, India Office to Foreign Office, 11 Aug. 1898 enclosing McMahon to Talbot, 10 May 1898. McMahon (later Sir Henry McMahon) produced a paper on the Hunza claims to Raskam and the Taghdumbash Pamir which is a full account of this complex subject as it was understood in 1898. For Raskam and the Taghdumbash Pamir, see Map 16.

marked the end of Hunza raids on the caravans, and the Hunza people then sought alternative means of livelihood. The fertile plots of Raskam, amounting to some 3000 acres in all, thus acquired a new importance in the Hunza economy. The Mir of Hunza maintained that the tracts had always formed part of his state, and had been recognised as such in his tributary relationship with the Chinese. To a ruler less land hungry than the Mir the Raskam district would have been scarcely worth troubling about. It was virtually uninhabited, having been depopulated by Hunza raids over the previous half century or more. Captain Deasy, who travelled through the area in 1897-98, has this to say about the object of the Mir's endeavours:

Raskam, with the exception of near Azgar, may be described as a narrow valley drained by the Yarkand River . . . . and is bounded by very high and barren mountains, which, for some distance east of Evgar, are very precipitous. Near Azgar the valley is broader, and the mountains on the south side rise up more gradually. Numerous patches of jungle, in which there is some high grass, are scattered about the valley . . . . while many ruins of houses, old irrigation channels, and fields no longer tilled, testify to Raskam having formerly been inhabited and cultivated. I have no doubt that if the small tributaries of the Yarkand River, as well as this river, are utilized for irrigation purposes, and labour expended on reclamation of land, a larger area than before could be cultivated remuneratively. The altitude varies from about 8,800 feet at Sarok Kamish to about 11,800 feet at Bazar Dara, which may be considered the eastern extremity of Raskam.[25]

In the spring of 1897 the Mir made a determined effort to open up the Raskam fields to the cultivation of his subjects. A small party of men was despatched to Azgar on the Yarkand to start the work. Some land was prepared, crops were sown, and then, because of difficulties of supply, all but two of the men returned to Hunza. The two who remained at Azgar were to watch and water the fields until harvest time, when they would again be reinforced from Hunza and the crops gathered in. At this point the Mir came into conflict with Chinese policy.[26]

In 1897 a new *Amban*, or Chinese district governor, of Yarkand was appointed. He appears to have been a man of energy and one who looked on the arable tracts of Raskam as potential areas for the settlement of Kirghiz nomads. No doubt something had to be done about the Kirghiz, whose freedom of movement had certainly been restricted by the Russian advances into the Pamirs and who had petitioned

[25] FO 539/81, No. 32 enclosing Deasy's narrative of 15 March 1898.
[26] The main source for the history of the Raskam crisis is the Foreign Office memorandum 'Precis of papers relating to rights of the Kanjutis in the Raskam Valley', dated Peking, Oct. 1903, which can be found as an enclosure in Satow to Lansdowne, 3 Nov. 1903 in FO 17/1600. I have made considerable use of this document in the following pages.

the Chinese for relief. In August or September 1897 the Yarkand *Amban* sent a party of Chinese officials to Raskam to look over the ground. When they came upon the two Hunza men at Azgar they promptly arrested them as trespassers on Chinese territory and sent them off under guard to the nearest Chinese post, probably Tashkurgan. After being held for six weeks, they were released. On learning of all this, the Yarkand *Amban* wrote to the Mir of Hunza explaining what had happened and issuing instruction that Hunza people should keep out of Raskam in the future. The Mir was both vexed and distressed. The crops which his subjects had planted were spoiled and their efforts were wasted.

To Macartney in Kashgar all this indicated that the Chinese were now giving the same attention to the western sector of their Karakoram frontier as they had already shown on the eastern sector in the neighbourhood of the Karakoram Pass. He had to hand other evidence to reinforce this conclusion. During 1897 two British travellers, Captain Deasy and Mr Cobbold, had been surveying and exploring in the Taghdumbash Pamir. They had experienced great difficulties in obtaining Chinese passports for this journey, and it appeared that the Kashgar authorities were unwilling to permit British travellers to remain in the Taghdumbash Pamir for more than ten days, which was tantamount to the granting of transit facilities only. Deasy and Cobbold had much trouble with the Chinese, who were then present in some force in the Taghdumbash Pamir and who objected strongly to the erection by the two Englishmen of stone pillars for survey purposes. The Chinese evidently thought that these were boundary pillars. The Kashgar *Taotai* asked Macartney to arrange for the prompt demolition of the pillars, hinting that if he did not do so the Chinese would remove them on their own responsibility. It was clear that the Chinese were about to initiate a campaign to establish their rights right up to the Hunza borders along the Karakoram watershed.

On learning of the fate of his two subjects at Azgar, the Mir of Hunza promptly despatched representatives to Kashgar to talk things over with the Chinese authorities. They arrived in November and at once put their case to Huang, the *Taotai*, who heard them out with some sympathy and reported in Hunza's favour to his superiors at Urumchi. The Hunza representatives do not seem to have made a claim to rights in Raskam, but to have confined themselves to a petition to the Chinese for permission to cultivate unused land in the Raskam area. The implication was clearly that Raskam was Chinese. To this petition Urumchi eventually returned a favourable reply. The Hunza people could cultivate a few Raskam plots if they so wished. At this point news of these events reached the ears of the Russian Consul in Kashgar, M. Petrovski, who immediately called upon the *Taotai* with a protest. In the interests of China, Petrovski declared, it would be unwise for two reasons to let the Hunza men establish a foothold in Raskam. First, Raskam was on the frontier, and the presence of the Hunza men there could have only an unsettling effect. Second, even if the Chinese allowed the Hunza people to settle in Raskam without actually ceding the tract to Hunza, the Mir would sooner or later come to look on it as his own, and the result would be, in effect, an advance of British territory because of the Mir's position within the political structure of British India. Thus almost from the outset the Raskam issue involved the Russians, and the fate of the two Hunza men at Azgar became the raw material of Anglo-Russian diplomacy.

Petrovski, who was an extremely shrewd observer of frontier matters, and who had, ever since the beginnings of the Pamirs crisis, been active in combating British influence in Kashgaria, undoubtedly saw the Hunza move into Raskam as the thin end of a British wedge. He was, in all probability, just as concerned at the prospect of the British turning the flank of the 1895 frontier line in the Pamirs as were the British at the prospect of a similar attempt by the Russians. His intervention in the Raskam affair greatly complicated the task of the Kashgar *Taotai*, who did not wish trouble with the British, yet who was impressed by the apparently greater power in Turkestan of the Russians. The *Taotai* proposed a compromise. He told Petrovski that it would indeed be most unwise to allow the Mir of Hunza any opportunity of looking on Raskam as anything but Chinese territory. He suggested therefore that the Hunza people should be allowed to settle in Raskam. 'The Chinese Government', he said, 'would be wanting in their duty if they failed to treat the Kanjutis [Hunza people] with kindness'. Nevertheless he would ensure that they were under no illusions that they owned the place by imposing on them a tax in grain. In effect, therefore, he proposed to rent Raskam to Hunza. The available evidence would suggest that Petrovski for the time being accepted this compromise. In April 1898 the Mir of Hunza's agent, Nazar Ali, was told the terms on which the Hunza men could come to Raskam, and he returned to Baltit, the Hunza capital, to report. The Mir thereupon made plans for the despatch of some 200 of his subjects to Azgar and other tracts in Raskam to start cultivation.

On 2 May 1898 Macartney called on the Kashgar *Taotai*, Huang, who said that he was 'glad to see the Raskam affair settled'. The *Taotai*, however, was being a bit premature. No sooner had news of the Chinese terms to Hunza leaked out than the Sarikolis of the Tashkurgan region, who had once paid taxes to Hunza, protested against the grant to Hunza of Raskam, which they themselves claimed and which they now petitioned the Chinese to allow them to cultivate. The

Chinese decided, once more, to compromise. They had originally, it seems, agreed to let Hunza have five plots in Raskam on the western bank of the Yarkand River. They would now make over but one plot, holding four in reserve until the conflicting Hunza and Sarikoli petitions could be resolved. Thus the Hunza people, when in late May 1898 they arrived in Raskam, found themselves offered one fifth of what they had anticipated. In June, after Hunza protests had reached Kashgar, a second plot was made over to them, and this was soon increased by further small grants. Eventually, after further representations by Nazar Ali, the entire area originally offered was promised to Hunza. The Chinese further agreed to waive for the time being the tax, or rent, on this land, and accepted the commutation of the grain tax for a sum in bullion, 10 seers of silver or its equivalent value in gold dust, which would be paid annually after a three or four year period of grace while the Hunza men brought their land into full production.

Petrovski was not very pleased when he saw the way in which the Raskam affair was developing. He evidently considered that the granting of any land in Raskam to Hunza was tantamount to a Chinese cession of Sinkiang territory to the British. With memories of Anglo-Chinese collusion in the period of the Pamirs crisis prior to the 1895 settlement, he may well have concluded that the British and the Kashgar authorities were again acting in concert. Raskam and the Taghdumbash Pamir probably appeared to him to be the route for a fresh British campaign against the Russian position in the Pamirs with, as its immediate objective, the long undefined stretch of Sino-Russian border between Pavalo-Schveikhovski Peak and the Uzbel Pass. Petrovski, therefore, let it be known that if the Hunza occupation of Raskam became an established fact, the Russians would have to seek a compensating extension of their own territory elsewhere. The obvious direction for such an extension, in view of the strategic background, was the northern Taghdumbash Pamir and Sarikol, the neighbourhood of Tashkurgan, or Tagarma as that place was sometimes called. Petrovski was in no way impressed by Chinese denials that any cession was involved and their references to the increased tribute which the Mir would have to pay. He no doubt noted that the fact that the Mir was already paying tribute for Hunza south of the watershed had not inhibited British freedom of action, and there was no reason to suppose that there would be any difference in Raskam.

The Sarikolis, who had petitioned for Raskam land, were likewise dissatisfied with the settlement. A party of them actually established itself in Raskam, and they continued, possibly with encouragement from Petrovski, to press the Chinese authorities to revoke in their favour the grant to Hunza. The

Chinese, faced with Sarikoli importunity and implied Russian threats, were extremely unhappy. They appreciated that to side with Hunza completely would, whatever they might argue to the contrary, be tantamount to siding with the British, and during the Pamirs crisis they had witnessed the failure of the British to check a Russian advance. The British were allies of doubtful reliability. Probably the Kashgar authorities decided that the best that they could do was to play for time, making the absolute minimum of concessions to Hunza, balancing these with concessions to the Sarikolis, and hoping that a solution would emerge which would not result in the determined application of either Russian or British pressure.

The development of the Raskam problem was watched closely by the British. The Indian Government received a stream of reports from the Political Agent at Gilgit, under whose wing Hunza was, and from Macartney at Kashgar. It is clear, however, that the actual genesis of the problem was in no way British inspired. The Mir of Hunza, now that he was prevented by the Indian Government from raiding the caravans, needed something else to keep his surplus population occupied and fed. He could turn only to agriculture, and the one direction in which he could seek more land to till was north of the watershed. Elsewhere he was hemmed in by other states under British protection the territory of which he could hardly hope to retain even if he managed to conquer them in some rapid campaign. This the British would never permit. Thus Raskam, where former rights had for some time been dormant, was his only outlet. Once embarked on his Raskam project, however, the Mir could hardly expect to be ignored by the British, since his claims involved a region which was becoming of considerable interest to strategists in both India and England. It was inevitable that a British attempt should be made to exploit the potentialities of Raskam in the effort to create a boundary between India and Sinkiang which the Russians, should they advance eastwards from the Pamirs, could not penetrate.

**The 1899 Proposals to China**

Sir John Ardagh's boundary proposals were made before the Raskam problem began to develop into a subject for Great Power diplomacy, and he was unaware of the extent of the Mir of Hunza's interests, which would have provided admirable arguments in support of his proposed alignment. Had the Indian Government accepted his proposals with all that they implied, it would have been logical for the British to back fully the Mir of Hunza in the Raskam question, thus staking at once their claim to a crucial tract within the new boundary. Lord Elgin's Government of India, however, did not accept Ardagh's proposals in full. They agreed

## II AKSAI CHIN AND THE RASKAM CRISIS: BOUNDARY DEFINITION IN THE KARAKORAM, 1895-1907

that some definite boundary to the north of Ladakh and Hunza should be settled with the Chinese in the near future, but they could not see that boundary as following Sir John Ardagh's line. They pointed out that the Chinese, whom Ardagh thought would give way easily enough, would certainly object to the surrender of any of the territory north of the watershed. The recent Chinese comments on their Aksai Chin tract being shown as British in the Johnstons' *Atlas* were examples of the attitude to be anticipated in Kashgar, Urumchi, and Peking. So also were the opening moves of the Raskam affair, of which the Government of India received reports while Ardagh's memorandum was still under consideration. Lord Elgin's Government noted on 23 December 1897 that

> we believe that any attempt to incorporate within our frontier either of the zones [i.e. Taghdumbash Pamir and Raskam and the Shahidulla-Suget region] mentioned by Sir John Ardagh would involve real risk of strained relations with China, and it might tend to precipitate the active interposition of Russia in Kashgaria, which it should be our aim to postpone as long as possible.

Moreover, Lord Elgin's Government continued,

> we are unable to concur altogether in Sir John Ardagh's suggestions on military grounds. He advocates an advance beyond the great mountain ranges which we regard as our natural frontier, on the ground that it is impossible to watch the actual watershed. Sir John Ardagh is no doubt right in theory, and the crest of a mountain range does not ordinarily form a good military frontier. In the present instance, however, we see no strategic advantage in going beyond mountains over which no hostile advance is ever likely to be attempted. . . Our objection is mainly based on the opinions of officers who have visited this region. They unanimously represent the present mountain frontier as perhaps the most difficult and inaccessible country in the world. The country beyond is barren, rugged, and sparsely populated. An advance would interpose between ourselves and our outposts a belt of the most difficult and impracticable country, it would unduly extend and weaken our military position without, in our opinion, securing any corresponding advantage. No invader has ever approached India from this direction where nature has placed such formidable barriers.[27]

These views the Indian Government saw no reason to modify during the course of 1898. In the spring of that year it was learnt that the Russians and Chinese, through the Chinese Minister in St Petersburg, had started a fresh round of discussions over the alignment of the Sino-Russian border in the Pamirs between Pavalo-Schveikhovski Peak and the Uzbel Pass (east of the Kara Kul Lake). It seemed more than likely that, at this juncture, a display of British interest in the possession of Raskam would induce the Russians to demand territory east of the Sarikol Range and to persuade the Chinese as to the wisdom of conceding it. But what if the Sino-

[27] FO 17/1356, Elgin to Hamilton No. 170 of 23 Dec. 1897, enclosed in India Office to Foreign Office 22 Jan. 1898.

43

Russian negotiations resulted, even without any British action in regard to Raskam, in a Chinese surrender of Sarikol and the Taghdumbash Pamir. As Captain (later Sir Henry) McMahon, the Political Agent at Gilgit, pointed out in May 1898, if Russia took over Sinkiang, or even if she merely annexed the Taghdumbash Pamir, she might well consider that she had also acquired China's rights over Hunza. In any case, the mere presence of the Russians to the immediate north of Hunza would have its political effects. Hunza needed room for expansion. Northwards lay the only possible direction. If Hunza had to look towards a Russian Raskam or Taghdumbash Pamir, then

Hunza would find that she had everything to expect from Russia and nothing from us. Human nature would lead her to make good terms with Russia at our expense. Our loss of prestige in Hunza, and loss of Hunza, for the latter must be considered the natural consequence of the former, would be felt throughout the whole country, and our position in Gilgit would become a very unpleasant one. Hunza is now so intimately connected with the other tribes of the Gilgit Agency, and those are so nearly connected with the people of Chitral, that trouble would not be confined to Gilgit only, but spread equally to Chitral. To shut one's eyes to these facts would be a foolish and dangerous proceeding.

From these arguments McMahon drew one conclusion. Like Ardagh, he felt that the northern slopes of the range must be kept within the British sphere, or, at least, prevented from ever passing into the Russian sphere. Like Ardagh and Macartney, McMahon thought that the absolute minimum requirement was the establishment of some reversionary right over Raskam and the Taghdumbash Pamir. The Chinese must not be allowed to alienate these districts to anyone but the Government of India.[28]

There was, of course, another solution possible for the Hunza problem. Instead of creating a buffer to its north so that the Russians would not be able to acquire the Chinese suzerainty over the Mir, why should not the Mir's relationship to China be severed once and for all? This step had been proposed during the Pamirs crisis, but had not been taken, largely in an effort to retain Chinese goodwill in a period when the British were relying on the Chinese to resist the Russian advance into the Pamirs. Now, perhaps, this goodwill was not so important. In any case, could it not still be retained by another use of the Mir's claims to Raskam and the Taghdumbash Pamir? As Lord Elgin telegraphed to Lord George Hamilton at the India Office on 20 July 1898, 'we might claim rights for Hunza over Taghdumbash and Raskam, but be prepared to renounce them in exchange for Chinese renunciation of all claims over Hunza. Our political control

[28] FO 17/1362, Capt. A. H. McMahon to Resident in Kashmir, 10 May 1898, in India Office to Foreign Office, 11 Aug. 1898.

over Hunza and Nagar is not relaxed'.[29] This was, in theory, clever diplomacy. The British would exchange something they did not, in effect, possess for something they very much wanted and which, also in effect, the Chinese did not possess. Just about this exchange was made the Sino-Pakistani boundary agreement of March 1963, though it was couched in rather different language. But would such an exchange work out in practice? Lord Elgin's Government certainly thought it worth the experiment.

Detailed proposals along these lines were submitted by the Indian Government on 27 October 1898. The crux of the matter, Lord Elgin appreciated, was the definition of the line of the boundary between what would be undoubted British territory, including Hunza, and what was to be recognised as territory falling under Chinese sovereignty. Such a line should not run north, except, perhaps, in one or two minor instances, of the main watershed. Such a line, moreover, would have to have an eastern as well as a western flank. The western flank, of course, had been provided by the Pamirs boundary laid down by the British and Russians in 1895, with its terminus at the Pavalo-Schveikhovski Peak. The eastern flank would have to be somewhere in the region of

[29]FO 17/1361, telegram from Elgin to Hamilton, 20 July 1898, in India Office to Foreign Office, 20 July 1898.

the Aksai Chin plateau. Lord Elgin's Government produced the following definition for such a line.

beginning at the north end of the peak Pavalo-Schveikovski, the line takes a south-easterly direction, crossing the Karachikar stream at Mintaka Aghazi, thence proceeding in the same direction till it joins, at the Karchanai Pass, the crest of the main ridge of the Mustagh range which it then follows passing the Khunjerab Pass and continuing southwards to the peak just north of the Shimshal Pass. At this point the boundary leaves the crest and follows a spur running east approximately parallel to the road from the Shimshal to the Hunza post at Darwaza. The line, turning south through the Darwaza post, crosses the road from the Shimshal Pass at that point and ascends the nearest high spur and regains the main crests, which the boundary will again follow, passing the Mustagh, Gusherbrum, and Saltoro Passes.

This was the section of the proposed line which related directly to the Hunza problem. Its definition, however, east of the Karakoram Pass was also required to link it to the eastern frontier between Ladakh and Tibet. This sector was defined as follows:

from the Karakoram Pass the crests of the range run nearly east for half a degree, and then turn south to a little below the 35th parallel of North Latitude. Rounding then what on our maps is shown as the source of the Karakash, the line of hills to be followed runs north-east to a point east of Kizil Jilga and from there, in a south-easterly direction, follows the Lak Tsung Range until that meets the spur running south from the Kuen Lun Range which has hitherto been shown on our maps as the eastern boundary of Ladakh. This is a little east of 80° East Longitude.

The Government of India regarded this definition as one which was based on natural features easily identified. They found themselves unable to plot the whole line on a map as they had no map at their disposal which was both reliable and extended eastwards on to the Aksai Chin plateau where cartography still relied very largely on the highly inaccurate survey by Johnson. The map that the Survey of India had prepared, at a scale of 1:1,000,000, to illustrate the travels of Captain Francis Younghusband was reasonably good from the Pamirs to the 79th meridian of east longitude, but further east it did not go. Nevertheless it was the best map available, and it was used to illustrate this and subsequent proposals. The eastward limitations of this map were dealt with in a rather unsatisfactory manner: a small extension beyond the right hand margin, based on Johnson's old survey, was added for the purpose of the present exercise so as to show the 'Lak Tsung Range until that meets the spur running south from the Kuen Lun Range'. The lack of a good map was not really serious, however, since it was proposed not that this boundary should actually be laid down on the ground, but that it should be offered to the Chinese as the border the British sought once the Chinese had given up their claims to rights to Hunza and the British, on behalf of Hunza, had given up claims to rights in those portions of Raskam and the Taghdumbash Pamir which fell to the north of the line.[30]

This line, it will be seen, followed the Indus-Tarim watershed from Pavalo-Schveikhovski Peak to the Karakoram Pass with two small deviations. At its starting point, instead of running around the head of the Karachukur River, as a watershed line should run, it cut across a portion of the Karachukur valley. This made a straighter line. It also made it possible for the line to start where the Pamirs Boundary Commission left off in 1895, because the watershed line would have had to start at the border of Afghan Wakhan a few miles southwest of Pavalo-Schveikhovski Peak and leaving, in consequence, a small tract of Sino-Afghan border undefined. In fact just this situation was to arise a few years later when, as we shall see, Lord Curzon brought the British line back to the watershed: and the resultant Sino-Afghan border was not to be formally delimited until the 1960s. Thus it could be argued that the inclusion on the British side of a small portion of the Taghdumbash Pamir had strategic advantages. It would prevent the Russians, should they ever take over Kashgaria, driving a wedge, as it were, between Wakhan and Hunza, a wedge pointed towards Chitral, and

[30] FO 17/1365, Elgin to Hamilton No. 198 of 27 Oct. 1898 in India Office to Foreign Office, 1 Dec. 1898. See Maps 13 and 14 for the Raskam area and the 1898-9 proposals for a boundary.

thus turning the flank of the carefully designed Wakhan buffer strip which was the geopolitical triumph of the 1895 Pamirs Boundary Commission.

A second departure from the watershed was in the region of Shimshal. Here, quite separate from the Raskam claims, there had long existed a Hunza outpost at Darwaza (or Darband). Younghusband saw it in 1889, and the Indian Government thought that it was still there in 1898. Clearly the Mir of Hunza was attached to this place, his possession of which had also been pointed to by Sir John Ardagh. It seemed reasonable to keep Darwaza on the British side, and it is worth noting in this context that here, in the Sino-Pakistani boundary agreement of 1963, the area of Pakistani occupation has been increased considerably when compared to the 1898 proposals.

To the east of the Karakoram Pass the watershed line is not so easy to determine. The main Karakoram Range swings southeast. The Kunlun Range is cut by the Karakash and Yarkand River systems. Wedged in between the Karakoram and Kunlun Ranges is a triangle of territory, the Aksai Chin and Lingzitang plateaus, which is really an extension of the vast wasteland of northern Tibet, a zone of internal drainages. The clearly defined watershed gets lost in this expanse of lakes without outlets. It may be followed between the Shyok and the Karakash, the one flowing into the Indus and the other into the Tarim basin; but at the head of the Karakash system, where it ends, there is a choice of watersheds separating internal drainage systems. The 1898 proposal, no doubt based on the claim to a Chinese Aksai Chin which the Kashgar *Taotai* had made to Macartney in 1896, leaves Aksai Chin, that is to say the Amtogor drainage basin, on the Chinese side. It follows the watershed which separates the Sarigh Jilganang basin from the Amtogor basin on the north (this line is what is meant by the Lak Tsung Range), and from the Nopte and Tsoggar basin on the east. The southern limit of the divide between the Sarigh Jilganang and Nopte-Tsoggar basins is the Lanak Pass, whence the frontier would follow the watershed at the head of the Changchenmo basin down to the Panggong Lake. This particular alignment avoids the awkward eastward pointing salient of the Changchenmo basin which would have resulted from the Trelawney Saunders alignment of 1873 which put Lingzitang as well as Aksai Chin on the Chinese or Tibetan side (if, indeed, a significant distinction could here be drawn between these two terms). In this sense the line proposed in 1898 was rather simpler to draw on maps than the 1873 suggestion. It also created a buffer between British and potentially Russian territory out of the fodderless Lingzitang plateau, which was to be recommended on strategic grounds.[31]

[31] See Maps 15 and 19.

The course of the 1898 proposal to the east of the Karakoram, as plotted on a modern map, has given rise in recent years to a certain amount of controversy, which has already been considered in the previous paper and need be touched on only briefly here. During their discussions with the Chinese in 1960-61 the Indian side repeated an interpretation first made in a letter in 1959 from Mr Nehru to Chou En-lai, namely that from the Karakoram Pass the line ran eastwards along the Kunlun Range to a point east of 80° east longitude. This, perhaps, arose from a misreading of the words: 'the spur running south from the Kuen Lun Range which has hitherto been shown on our maps as the eastern boundary of Ladakh. This is a little east of 80° East Longitude'. The omission of the word 'spur' leads to a very different reading; and this mistake the Indian side, in their haste to gather ammunition against the Chinese, may have made. Moreover, if the line of the 1898 proposal, following the watersheds indicated above, is plotted on a modern map it does not, in fact, meet the eastern Ladakh border to the east of 80° east longitude: it meets it just to the west of that meridian.[32] This fact arises from errors in the original survey by Johnson in 1865, which continued to be copied by the Survey of India throughout the rest of the nineteenth century—they finally begin to be corrected in about 1906—which placed the watershed of the Sarigh Jilganang basin further to the east than has subsequently been shown to be the case. The correction in the Johnson survey, oddly enough, has not always resulted in a corresponding correction in the alignment of the frontier between India and Tibet. The frontier now claimed by India, for example, is described verbally as following the watershed yet, by its co-ordinates, actually crosses a limb of the Nopte basin. The same set of co-ordinates would have produced a watershed line on a nineteenth century map. Some modern maps, therefore, which show a watershed frontier, do not agree exactly with the Indian claim. A good example is the United States Army Map Service edition of the Asia 1:1,000,000 series Sheet N.I.44. Defects in maps available to the Government of India in 1898 have certainly resulted in much subsequent confusion. (See Map 8.)

The boundary proposed by the Government of India in October 1898 was put to the Tsungli Yamen, the Chinese Foreign Office of the day, on 14 March 1899 in a note presented by Sir Claude MacDonald, the British Minister at Peking. It is a document which makes interesting reading, and it merits study in detail.[33]

[32] A more detailed elaboration of this particular argument has already been made in the previous chapter.
[33] FO 17/1373, despatch No. 81 of 7 Apr. 1899 from Bax-Ironside to Foreign Office enclosing Sir Claude MacDonald to the Tsung-li Yamen, 14 March 1899. The text of this note is printed in Lamb, *China-India Border*, op. cit., pp. 180-2 and in Woodman, op. cit., pp. 366-7.

MacDonald's note opened with an explanation of how the British came to be so interested in Hunza (or Kanjut), which was described as a tributary of Kashmir and a region whose ruler's 'rebellious conduct' had had to be repressed by force in 1891. Despite this action on the part of the British, however, the Chinese continued to assert their claim to the 'allegiance' of Hunza on the basis of the tribute of $1\frac{1}{2}$ ounces of gold dust which the Mir paid to the authorities in Sinkiang each year. The boundary between Hunza and China, MacDonald continued, had 'never been clearly defined'. The Mir claimed 'an extensive tract of land in the Taghdumbash Pamir, extending as far north as Tashkurgan', and he also claimed 'the district known as Raskam to the south of Sarikol'. From 1896 these two tracts had been the subject of discussion between the Mir and the Chinese; and MacDonald pointed out that the Chinese had admitted that land in Raskam should be given to the Hunza people. For reasons arising from these discussions

it is now proposed by the Indian Government that for the sake of avoiding any dispute or uncertainty in the future, a clear understanding should be come to with the Chinese Government as to the frontier between the two States. To obtain this clear understanding, it is necessary that China should relinquish her shadowy claims over the State of Kanjut [Hunza]. The Indian Government, on the other hand, will, on behalf of Kanjut, relinquish her claims to most of the Taghdumbash and Raskam districts.

Thus MacDonald was proposing a straight exchange of Chinese claims over Hunza for Hunza claims over 'most' of the Taghdumbash and Raskam. So far, contrary to what several later commentators have written, Aksai Chin was not involved in the transaction. To formalise the exchange, a boundary between British India and China, MacDonald next observed, should be agreed upon. 'It will not be necessary', he said, 'to mark out the frontier' because 'the natural frontier is the crest of a range of mighty mountains, a great part of which is quite inaccessible': all that was called for was a joint Anglo-Chinese recognition of 'the frontier as laid down by its clearly marked geographical features', which boundary MacDonald then described verbally just as it had been described by the Government of India in October 1898. His only addition to the wording was to explain 'half a degree' as being equal to 100 Chinese *li*. In conclusion, MacDonald remarked that 'Your Highnesses and Your Excellencies [of the Tsungli Yamen] will see by examining this line that a large tract of country to the north of the great dividing range shown on Hung Chün's map as outside the Chinese boundary will be recognised as Chinese territory'. Thus an attempt was made, though certainly with no great conviction, to argue that the British abandonment of claims to Shahidulla and Suget, as well as to the Aksai Chin plateau, represented a concession. It was a point which the note did not labour.

The British note of 14 March 1899 represents, so far as the available records show, the only formal proposal on a boundary between India and China in the Karakoram, that is to say from Wakhan to the Lanak Pass at the head of the Changchenmo basin, which the British ever made to the Chinese during the course of their rule in India. As such it is clearly an extremely important document with some bearing on the alignment of the Sino-Indian border when it became subject to Chinese challenge in the 1950s.[34]

The Tsungli Yamen, as was its wont in such cases, volunteered no prompt reply to MacDonald's note, but information reaching Macartney in Kashgar showed that it had sent the details of the proposed boundary to the Sinkiang Government in Urumchi which had reported favourably on it. Unfortunately, perhaps, for the future peace of Ladakh, the Tsungli Yamen did not quite understand the implications of MacDonald's words. Possibly the Chinese version contained ambiguities absent in the original. At all events, the Yamen somehow concluded that the note constituted a British *claim* to Raskam and the Taghdumbash Pamir rather than an offer to waive all claims to those tracts. There is, of course, a certain sense behind such an interpretation since the very acceptance of the British waiver of claims was an admission that these claims had once existed, and the exchange of Chinese claims over Hunza, the validity of which the Yamen did not doubt for one moment, for British claims could be construed to mean that up to the moment when the transaction was completed British claims on behalf of Hunza were in fact valid. Hence, if the Chinese agreed to open discussions on the basis of MacDonald's note, and these discussions then failed to produce an agreement signed and sealed, would not the Chinese find that they had, in effect, validated the Hunza claims which, in these circumstances, would remain in being? Such, at all events, could well have been the working of the Chinese mind, always prone to seek out the subtle pitfalls of any proposition. It must be admitted that the wording of the note did leave openings for such a construction, and that the British, in the event of failure of the negotiations, would certainly cling on to the bargaining power of the Mir of Hunza's claims. The Chinese were probably reluctant, on principle, to admit the validity of any foreign claims over what they considered to be their territory,

---

[34] Recent writers like Neville Maxwell, whose *India's China War* has already been noted, make it clear that it is difficult to overemphasise the importance of the Aksai Chin question in the genesis of the Sino-Indian argument of the 1950s and 1960s. The most dramatic armed conflict in 1962 may have taken place along the McMahon Line tract of the Assam Himalaya many thousands of miles to the east but, in Chinese eyes at least, the major territorial concern was Aksai Chin across which ran the Sinkiang-Tibet motor road. In any discussion of the Aksai Chin question one cannot ignore either the 1899 note or its misquotation in recent times.

even in the most indirect way. In this particular instance, however, they had a further inducement to be cautious. Anything which could be interpreted as a cession to the British of Sinkiang territory, the Russians had hinted broadly enough, would lead to the Russians seeking compensating concessions. Thus an incautious initiation of Anglo-Chinese discussions on the basis of MacDonald's note might well, perhaps the Tsungli Yamen thought, lead to nothing but a Russian occupation of the Tashkurgan district in Sarikol which, in turn, might be the prelude for further Russian advances towards the heart of Kashgaria. The logic behind this kind of reasoning became clearer in the months that followed the presentation of MacDonald's note, when the Raskam problem developed a stage further.

### The Raskam Crisis: second phase

By the end of 1898 the Raskam question had reached a state of uneasy compromise. The Mir was in token occupation of a few plots, but the massive cultivation which he had planned for the 1898 season had had to be postponed when the Chinese started having second thoughts about the quantity of land which he might hold. During the winter of 1898-99 negotiations took place between Nazar Ali, the Mir's representative, and the Chinese as to the exact terms on which Raskam land could be held and the necessary upward revision of the Mir's tribute. Nazar Ali, in the course of these discussions, pressed for more land in Raskam than the five plots on the west bank of the Yarkand which the Chinese were offering, pointing out that the Mir was fully entitled to Azgar on the east bank where, in the days before Yakub Bey, the Hunza people had built a fort and other structures, the ruins of which could still be seen. Had not the Raskam affair become increasingly one of international interest, there can be little doubt that by the end of 1899 a settlement would have been signed and sealed and the Hunza people, in the 1900 season, could have started in earnest the work which the Mir had originally planned for 1898. The Russians, however, intervened.

Petrovski, the Russian Consul in Kashgar, had been watching closely and reporting back to Tashkent on the progress of the talks between Nazar Ali and the Chinese. He evidently concluded that the Chinese tendency was towards some concessions to Hunza, which the Russians ought to oppose. So also thought his superiors in the Turkestan Government-General. In late January or early February 1899 Petrovski was instructed to inform the Kashgar *Taotai* that if the Hunza people obtained what they sought in Raskam the Russians would have no alternative but to demand the right to establish posts in Sarikol in the neighbourhood of Tashkurgan. Shortly afterwards the *Taotai* was informed by telegraph that the Tsungli Yamen in Peking had derived from other sources a similar picture of Russian policy on the Raskam question. The *Taotai* in these circumstances and with the approval of Urumchi decided to put off the Mir's occupation of any Raskam tracts for the time being.[35]

What had been going on? Had the Russians, both in Kashgar and in Peking, been threatening the Chinese; or had the Chinese merely taken alarm at the thought of what the Russians might do and acted as it were, in unprovoked anticipation? The British had no doubt that there had been the application of Russian pressure. The *Taotai* convinced Macartney that the Russian Minister at Peking had been pressing the Tsungli Yamen in the same manner as Petrovski had the Kashgar authorities. If so, then the Raskam affair had thereby escalated to a higher diplomatic level. Lord Salisbury at the Foreign Office in London decided to instruct Sir Charles Scott, the British Ambassador at St Petersburg, to make an informal approach to Count Mouraviev at the Russian Foreign Ministry on the subject. Mouraviev denied that there had been any Russian pressure. The question was one which concerned China and India only. He would countenance no Russian threats. He was not aware that the Russians had any intention, under any circumstances, of occupying territory in Sarikol.

Mouraviev's observations were reported to Bax-Ironside, who was then British *chargé* at Peking. Bax-Ironside relayed them to the Tsungli Yamen, which had no hesitation in warning the British diplomat not to take too seriously the Russian's statements. The Tsungli Yamen were evidently much perturbed at the way things were going in Kashgaria since they knew that China could not possibly hope to hold a successful balance between Russia and England once serious competition developed. Their only policy was to avoid all causes of such competition, and for this reason they begged Bax-Ironside to let Raskam alone for a while. After all, they said, no definite agreement had yet been entered into which committed China to letting the Mir cultivate in Raskam; the matter was still under negotiation. Bax-Ironside, however, was unable to let the Yamen exploit this escape route, since there had been no doubt that the Sinkiang authorities had made a definite offer to Hunza, as the Kashgar *Taotai* had admitted to Macartney on more than one occasion. It was clearly out of the question for the Indian Government to permit its subjects to be deprived of their rights in response to Russian pressure. The Yamen then observed that the big stumbling block in the matter was the Russians. At that

---

[35] FO 17/1600, Satow to Lansdowne, 3 Nov. 1903 enclosing 'Precis of papers relating to rights of the Kanjutis in the Raskam Valley'. This is, as has already been noted, a most valuable summary of the British documents relating to the Raskam problem.

moment a Sino-Russian border in the Pamirs was being negotiated; and anything which the Russians could possibly interpret as a Chinese surrender of territory to the British would produce, automatically, stiffer Russian terms. If the Chinese let the Mir have what he asked for in Raskam, there could be no doubt that the Russians would take over Sarikol. Since this was by far the greater evil, the Yamen hoped that Bax-Ironside would understand why they could not be more helpful to the British in this matter.[36]

By the end of June the Russian attitude in St Petersburg seemed to be hardening. Perhaps Mouraviev had received more information from Kashgar, Tashkent, and Peking; perhaps, he had merely had more time for reflection. On 28 June he told Hardinge that he certainly could not authorise the Russian Minister in Peking to press the Chinese Government to comply with the Mir of Hunza's request, and thus give the lie to the prevailing impression of active Russian opposition to Hunza cultivation in Raskam.[37] He needed much more information as to the area of land in Raskam which was involved. Mouraviev, so Hardinge reported to London, observed that

the Government of India had of late been rapidly pushing forward, and had made a considerable advance northwards on the side of the frontier of Kashgar, that they had even pushed towards Sari Kol in the direction of the Russian outposts, and that a carriage road was about to be, or was actually being, constructed from a point within the Indian frontier, the name of which he had forgotten, to Yarkand.

Mouraviev, Hardinge went on, added that

he wished to point out, which he proceeded to do by means of a rough sketch, that the Russian position in the Pamirs was, in consequence of such steps, in danger of being outflanked and turned. He declared that he was very anxious that the relative positions of Russia and England in Central Asia as settled by the Pamirs Convention should be maintained, but that any movement of the Government of India, such as he had received information of, would be considered to modify the situation created by the Pamirs Convention, and that the Russian Government would be compelled to seek compensation for the encroachments of the Indian Government towards the north. He added that he believed Her Majesty's Government were no parties to such measures, but that the officers on the Indian frontier were enterprising, and that it was difficult for Her Majesty's Government to know what was going on.

Of course, as Hardinge quickly pointed out, there were no British carriage roads then under construction towards Yarkand. Mouraviev had produced a garbled version of recent British exploration across the Karakoram, journeys like those of Deasy and Cobbold to which reference has already been made, combined with a memory of British plans for trade

---

[36] FO 539/81, No. 4, Bax-Ironside to Salisbury, 29 May 1899.
[37] FO 539/81, No. 1, Hardinge to Salisbury, 28 June 1899.

routes to Yarkand in the Yakub Bey era. However, Mouraviev also gave an interesting picture of Russian sensitivity on the Pamirs flank, and it looked as if he had been listening to some Russian equivalent of Sir John Ardagh.

A similar picture of Russian attitudes was obtained on 9 June 1899 by Lieutenant-Colonel MacSwiney, a British soldier then engaged on a journey through Russia to India, from no less a personage than General Kuropatkin, the Russian Minister of War.[38] During a call on the General at his country house, MacSwiney brought the conversation round to Kashgaria and the Raskam question. He assured the General that there was absolutely no truth in the story of carriage roads from British territory to Kashgar, though it was just possible that the Hunza people might have made a beaten track to the fields in Raskam which they hoped to till. The General replied: 'if your Kanjutis go into Raskam, we shall be forced to take over Kashgar, Tashkurgan, &c., which, as a young Captain, in my report on Kashgar, I strongly advised my Government not to do'. MacSwiney said he was rather surprised that the General could 'in any way regard the few Kanjuti agriculturalists in Raskam as a military occupation of Chinese territory'. General Kuropatkin replied: 'all the same, it disturbs us'.[39]

Once the Russians had taken this attitude, the Indian Government felt increasingly reluctant to precipitate a Kashgarian crisis of the proportions now threatened. At the same time, it could hardly forget all about Raskam and the proposals already made to China concerning the Hunza claims north of the watershed. For one thing, the more indications the Russians gave of an impending advance into Kashgaria, the more important it was to obtain a settled Indian border, and the entire question of the border alignment had, in MacDonald's note of 14 March 1899, been tied to the Hunza and Taghdumbash Pamir questions. The whole situation seemed to be a bit confused. On the one hand, the Mir of Hunza was pressing his Chinese suzerain to give him concessions in Raskam, which the Chinese regarded as part of their territory, and the Mir was receiving a significant measure of British diplomatic support. On the other hand, the British were proposing to waive the Mir's claims over Raskam, at least in matters of sovereignty. It was evident that the Chinese, or so the Indian Government concluded, saw in what was essentially a moderate, or static, British policy the nucleus of a British forward move. Perhaps, if Bax-Ironside explained it all more clearly to the Yamen, the Chinese might modify their attitude. This, however, proved to be a vain hope. The

---

[38] FO 539/81, No. 6, Scott to Salisbury, 12 July 1899.

[39] Kanjuti was a term commonly used in the nineteenth century to refer to the inhabitants of Hunza, which some travel accounts used to call Hunza Kanjut.

Yamen left Bax-Ironside in no doubt that it did not really matter what British policy was. The key to the Chinese outlook lay in their interpretation of Russian policy. They might think that Britain was being extremely reasonable; but they also knew that the Russians were not. Subtle distinctions between sovereignty rights and cultivation rights were unlikely to impress the Russians.

At this juncture, in late May or June 1899, the Chinese in Kashgaria endeavoured to cut the Gordian knot by informing the Mir of Hunza that, as a result of discussions between the Tsungli Yamen and the British and Russian representatives in Peking, it had been decided that the Hunza people could not, after all, cultivate any land in Raskam. If the Chinese thought that this would bring the Raskam question to a close, they were very much mistaken.

It was obvious to the British that the key to the problem lay in Russia. If St Petersburg could be persuaded to agree with the British position over Raskam, then the Chinese would follow suit. In August 1899, therefore, another effort was made to bring round Count Mouraviev. He was given precise details of the area involved in the Hunza Raskam claims, no more than 3000 acres, and the precise nature of the cultivation rights sought by Hunza was explained in great detail. On 22 August Mouraviev told Sir Charles Scott that he was satisfied that the British were not seeking fresh territory in Raskam and that he now understood fully the nature of the Mir's claims, which involved only seeking from the Chinese permission to cultivate. Hence, Mouraviev said, he would now instruct the Russian Minister in Peking, M. de Giers, to cease to apply pressure on the Yamen.[40] By the beginning of September M. de Giers had acted on these instructions and on 2 September the Tsungli Yamen promised Bax-Ironside that they would at once telegraph to Kashgar to authorise the *Taotai* to carry out the engagements which he had made with Hunza over cultivation in Raskam.[41] This was done on 27 September; and it looked as if the Raskam affair was over.

The Kashgar authorities, however, were still under pressure. The Russian Consulate General continued to advise against the wisdom of letting the Hunza men into Raskam, hinting at the compensation they would seek elsewhere and pointing out the trouble that was bound to arise between Hunza and the disappointed Sarikolis who still sought Raskam lands as well. The Kashgar *Taotai*, apparently with the approval both of Urumchi and Peking, decided to play for yet more time and to postpone the completion of the lease of Raskam land to Hunza for a while more. Sir Charles Scott, in January 1900, asked Mouraviev what all this meant, and

[40] FO 539/81, No. 27, Scott to Salisbury, 22 Aug. 1899.
[41] FO 538/81, No. 31, Bax-Ironside to Salisbury, 3 Sep. 1899.

Mouraviev replied, perhaps a trifle evasively, that the Raskam question was a matter concerning the Chinese only, and that the Russian Consul General at Kashgar, Petrovski, 'not being supplied with the requisite powers', could not protest against 'the transfer to the Kanjutis of lands near Raskam for temporary use'.[42] The Tsungli Yamen, when MacDonald informed them of Mouraviev's views, did not feel that the problem had really been very much clarified. The Yamen, MacDonald reported, pointed out that

> although the Russian Government disavowed the opposition of their Consul to the arrangement regarding this land [Raskam], they gave no assurance as to not making counter-claims; and there was little doubt that any concession to Hunza would be made the basis of territorial claims on China, the nature and extent of which it would be impossible to foresee. The position of the Chinese Government in this matter ... was one of great difficulty.[43]

Such remained the Chinese attitude for the rest of 1900. They would defer a final decision on the Raskam question: meanwhile, the Mir should be patient and not try to cultivate the Raskam lands to which he thought he was entitled.

By 1900 Lord Curzon had replaced Lord Elgin as Viceroy and, for this reason alone, one would have expected an intensification of British activity in support of the Hunza claims. It may well have been the presence of Curzon that decided the Russians to keep up their pressure on the Chinese to keep the Hunza men out. There can be little doubt, at all events, that Curzon paid a closer attention, interested in Central Asian affairs as he was, to Raskam than had his predecessor. He may well have given thought to a more forceful demonstration of British support to the Mir, perhaps even the provision of a British escort to the Hunza cultivators in Raskam. From the outset of his administration he saw in Raskam a Russian challenge to British prestige. As he wrote to Lord George Hamilton, the Secretary of State for India, on 10 May 1899:

> I do not suppose we should back up the Hunza people because the lands to which they are laying claim have anything to do with our frontier—as a matter of fact they lie outside it; but because they are lands to which Hunza has a *bona fide* claim; over which China, who exercises a sort of overlordship in these districts, has been willing voluntarily to admit her rights; which she has occupied and cultivated more or less regularly for half a century; and which are essential for the expansion of her already much straitened population. That a bargain of this sort should be cancelled at the last moment owing to the bluster of Petrovski at Kashgar, and the threats of the Russian Minister at Peking, is, I think, quite inexcusable. Nor do I understand the reluctance of the Foreign Office to approach the Russian Government about an action so obviously unfriendly. If we do not stand by the Hunza men in a case where right is so obviously on their side, we shall give them

---

[42]FO 539/83, No. 9, Scott to Salisbury, 10 Jan. 1900.
[43]FO 539/83, No. 46, MacDonald to Salisbury, 1 March 1900.

the impression that Russia has only to threaten in order to carry the day, and shall forfeit much of the respect upon which on the confines of Empire power so largely depends. Had any one of our officials adopted an attitude one tenth as compromising in respect of Russian interests in any part of the world, I do not hesitate to say that M. de Staal [the Russian Ambassador in London] would immediately have been closeted with Lord Salisbury.[44]

In this characteristic passage Lord Curzon revealed that his thoughts had been dwelling on measures which might well have resulted in a British military occupation of the northern slopes of the Karakoram Range, and which could, perhaps, have eventually produced an Ardagh type boundary settlement. However, it is certain that Curzon appreciated that the situation did not really call for such powerful expedients. Sinkiang was beyond the British border and on the fringes of the Russian sphere. It was a direction where the British could not possibly hope to advance. A valiant rearguard action was more likely the wisest policy. In 1900, with the outbreak of the Boxer rising and the threatened total collapse of China, it seemed even less probable that Kashgaria could be saved from a determined Russian attempt to grab it, and by this time Curzon's attention was becoming focused on Afghanistan and Tibet, where Russian advances would be far more detrimental to British interests than they could possibly be in Sinkiang. There is in the flood of Curzonian warnings on the Raskam danger a certain lack of conviction which we cannot detect in the documents of the growing Tibetan crisis where the Viceroy was in deadly earnest.

However, the Raskam crisis developed in such a manner as to make it extremely unlikely that Lord Curzon would favour any solution which did not involve the abandonment of Russian opposition, overt and covert, to the Hunza cultivation north of the watershed. He thought, he told Hamilton, that 'the whole affair is a plot organised by Petrovski in Kashgar to aggrandise himself at the expense of British influence', and he hoped that 'Her Majesty's Government will not allow themselves to be bluffed by this unscrupulous braggart'.[45] Against Petrovski Lord Curzon advocated the use of a weapon which the Indian Government had so far been doing its best to discard, namely the assertion of Hunza, and hence British, sovereignty over Raskam and the Taghdumbash Pamir. This, Curzon thought, 'would be more than the Russians had bargained for, and would probably bring them to their senses'. Hence, under Curzon, there was a certain reluctance to agree to a unilateral abandonment of the trans-Karakoram tracts and the formal acceptance of the

[44] India Office Eur. M.S.S. D 510/1, Curzon to Hamilton, 10 May 1899.

[45] India Office Eur. M.S.S. D 510/2, Curzon to Hamilton, 23 Aug. 1899.

boundary proposed in 1898-99 until the Mir's cultivation rights had been guaranteed.

The Russians, perhaps sensing the direction in which Curzon's thoughts were moving, maintained their resistance to the Hunza rights. Under pressure from Petrovski the Kashgar *Taotai* continued to defer his final settlement with the Mir's agent, Nazar Ali. Meanwhile, he issued orders that the Hunza men were not to be allowed into Raskam to till the fields and, it would seem, he began to encourage the settling in the Raskam area of those Sarikolis who had for some time been pestering him for permission to do this. It is not clear from the documents quite how extensive the *Taotai*'s prohibition was. Did it apply to the plots on the west bank of the Yarkand, which had been offered to the Mir in 1898, or did it merely relate to those east bank tracts, like Azgar, which the Mir sought in addition to the original Chinese grant? Some of the British papers on Raskam from 1901 onwards give the impression that the Mir's cultivation had been stopped completely, yet other evidence suggests that throughout the first decade of the twentieth century some Hunza cultivators continued working across the main watershed.

In addition to their opposition to the Hunza claims, by 1901 the Russians had finally decided upon another step, one with potentially quite serious implications. They sought from the Kashgar authorities the lease of a plot of land near Tashkurgan, that is to say in Sinkiang just over the *de facto* Sino-Russian border along the Sarikol Range, where they proposed to establish a small military outpost, manned by a Russian officer, four Cossacks, and six native troops. The post, which came under the direct administration of the Russian Consulate General at Kashgar, was justified as being required to protect the Russian postal route between Kashgar and Russian Turkestan. Curzon, naturally enough, interpreted the Tashkurgan post as the beginning of further Russian advance in the Pamirs. 'If we mildly acquiesce', he protested to Hamilton, 'in Russian advances over the Taghdumbash and Sarikol, we shall find them cheek by jowl with us on the Hindu-Kush before we know where we are'.[46] He urged a protest in St Petersburg, and added that he was 'quite prepared to send a British officer from time to time to Taghdumbash to vindicate our joint interests'.[47] In London, however, neither the fresh Raskam development nor the Russian post appeared quite so alarming as Lord Curzon made out. Indeed, the India Office was already

[46]India Office Eur. M.S.S. D 510/8, Curzon to Hamilton, 1 May 1901.

[47]India Office Secret and Political Department confidential memorandum A 160, quoting telegram from Curzon to Hamilton, 13 March 1901.

beginning to see the wisdom of taking with a grain of salt the dreadful consequences which the Viceroy tended to prophesy would arise from small happenings on remote frontiers. They certainly had enough evidence of the Curzonian cast of mind in the growing Tibetan storm which was being stirred up by the arrival in Russia of missions claiming to represent the Dalai Lama at the same time as that ruler had been refusing to receive any communications at all from the Government of India. As far as the reported expulsion of Hunza people from Raskam was concerned, the India Office thought that a note might be addressed to the Chinese Government. However, 'as regards the [Russian] post established with the consent of the Chinese at Tashkurgan', Sir Arthur Godley of the India Office noted to the Foreign Office, 'there appears to be no *locus standi* for any remonstrance in reference to a post so far removed from our frontier'. Thus the only British action at this stage was to protest to the Chinese.[48] Sir Ernest Satow, the British Minister at Peking, addressed notes to the Chinese Government on 29 May and 28 November 1901, in which he requested that Peking instruct Kashgar to allow the Hunza men to cultivate those fields in Raskam which the Chinese had already promised them on more than one occasion. The Chinese, after much delay, promised to look into the matter. The Sinkiang Provincial Government, Prince Ch'ing (of the Wai-wu-pu, the Chinese Foreign Ministry which had been set up immediately after the Boxer crisis to take the place of the Tsungli Yamen, a body much disliked by European diplomats) informed Satow on 26 February 1902, would be told to report immediately. Here, Prince Ch'ing evidently hoped, the matter would end.[49]

On 14 January 1903, however, the Russian *chargé* in London, Baron Graevenitz, presumably under instructions from St Petersburg, took steps to keep the Raskam pot mildly simmering.[50] He delivered a note to Lord Lansdowne, the British Foreign Secretary, in protest against the terms of Satow's notes to the Chinese of May and November 1901 on the Raskam issue. The British notes, Baron Graevenitz pointed out, implied a British claim to sovereignty over Raskam; and such claims Sir Charles Scott had denied in his talks with Mouraviev when the Raskam problem first developed. Lansdowne had no choice but to reply that 'Her Majesty's Government made no claim on behalf of the Mir of Hunza to territorial rights, but merely to cultivation and

[48] Loc. cit., quoting India Office to Foreign Office, 23 March 1901.
[49] Foreign Office confidential print 8280, No. 37, Satow to Lansdowne, 23 March 1902.
[50] Foreign Office confidential print 8263, No. 12, memorandum by Lansdowne, 22 Jan. 1903.

proprietary rights', an admission which took all the sting out of the kind of policy which Curzon would have liked to follow, in which the Mir's Raskam rights were, at least for temporary diplomatic purposes, converted into a full blooded British territorial claim. Even the word 'proprietary', after its implications had been questioned by Count Benckendorff, the Russian Ambassador in London, was so defined by Lansdowne as to deprive it of any implication of Hunza sovereignty. Thus, the British border in the Hunza region was in a sense, defined by these exchanges between Lansdowne and the Russians, as, indeed, it had also been during the Mouraviev-Scott exchanges. The British border was the border between Hunza proper and Sinkiang. It did not embrace either Raskam or the Taghdumbash Pamir. It followed, in other words, the line, more or less, of the main watershed, just as the British had defined it in the note to China of 14 March 1899. In these circumstances it would have been logical enough for the British to attempt to secure from China a formal recognition of this particular boundary line, leaving the final settlement of the Raskam problem for another day. In one sense this did become British policy, but, as we shall see, there were a number of practical difficulties which made it hard for the British to accept the full implications of this line of policy.

## The 1899 Boundary: some later stages

There were two main objections to pressing the Chinese for a reply to MacDonald's note of 14 March 1899. First, the boundary agreement it contained would have involved the British in an absolutely final renunciation of any claim, on behalf of their Hunza subjects, to an interest in Raskam and the Taghdumbash Pamir. Even if Lansdowne had emphasised to the Russians the absence of Hunza, and hence British, territorial rights here, it still might be possible, if the Russians developed further their foothold at Tashkurgan, to find some bargaining value in these trans-Karakoram tracts. The full extent of the Russian intentions at Tashkurgan were as yet unknown. As Macartney asked the Kashgar *Taotai* in June 1902, what limit had there been placed, if any, on the number of troops which the Russians proposed to station and the size of the permanent buildings they proposed to erect there?[51] No one knew. Should the Russian post at Tashkurgan blossom into something like a military colony, then it was clear that the British would at least have to think about setting up a similar establishment of their own in the Taghdumbash Pamir and it would be far easier for them to extract the necessary concessions from the Chinese if the boundary had not been finally settled.

[51] Foreign Office confidential print 8280, No. 69.

A second reason was to be found in the growing British conviction that the 1899 proposals did not go far enough. The great obstacle to British influence in Kashgaria was the Russian Consulate General. So long as the British representative in Kashgar was deprived of full Consular status he was in no position to offer an effective challenge to the Russians. Since at least 1900 Macartney had concluded that the prime British aim in Sinkiang should be the establishment there of a British Consulate, and the creation of the Russian post at Tashkurgan appears to have given greater weight to Macartney's views in the eyes of the Home Government. It seemed logical, therefore, that added to the settlement proposed in 1899 should be the question of a British Consulate in Kashgar. In the event, the negotiations on this question somehow became separated from the boundary problem. When Macartney was finally recognised by the Chinese as a Consul, in 1908, the boundary was not discussed. Indeed, by the time Macartney, knighted and with the rank of Consul General, finally retired from Kashgar at the end of the First World War, the boundary question appears to have assumed an extremely low position on the agenda of pressing topics of Sino-British discussion relating to Sinkiang.

A third reason was that the Indian Government had ceased to be entirely satisfied with the boundary proposed in the 1899 note. By 1904 Lord Curzon had decided that no amount of protest in Peking was going to get for the Mir his fields in Raskam. He proposed, therefore, that the Chinese should be told forthwith that the Mir would from henceforth cease to pay any tribute to them and that their claims to any suzerain rights over Hunza were now at an end. The Raskam and Taghdumbash claims would be abandoned, and the Mir would be compensated by the annual payment of a small sum, perhaps 3000 rupees. Lord Curzon concluded:

we accordingly recommend that a formal notification be made to China that since the Chinese Government have been unable to fill their promises to the Mir of Hunza, that State, under the advice of the British Government, withdraws from all relations with China, and henceforth will owe suzerainty to the Kashmir State and the British Government alone. As regards the boundary between Kashmir and the New Dominion, we strongly recommend that the Chinese Government should be informed that, as they have not shown any reasons for disagreeing with the proposals placed before them in Sir Claude MacDonald's despatch of the 14th March, 1899, we shall henceforth assume Chinese concurrence and act accordingly.[52]

So far the Indian Government appears to have been committed to an unconditional unilateral implementation of the 1899

[52]PSF 1912/82, India Office Political Department confidential memorandum A 170 of 1911, 'Frontier between Hunza and the Chinese Dominions', Part II. This memorandum is a most useful summary of the later stages of the Raskam question and their consequences.

note. However, it soon transpired that this was easier said than done. Apart from a British reluctance to let go of the Taghdumbash Pamir so long as the Russian post at Tashkurgan remained in being and continued to grow in size—by 1904 there were twenty-two men there, Macartney reported —it was discovered that the Mir was unlikely to accept the loss, even when compensated in cash, of his Raskam claims. The least that could be done, Curzon came to believe, was to increase a little the extent of Hunza territory across the Shimshal Pass. By 1905, therefore, the 1899 boundary came to be modified slightly, a fact which, no doubt, made it harder to establish by unilateral declaration. Some fresh approach to the Chinese would be called for and this, inevitably, tied up the boundary question with that of the Kashgar Consulate.

The Shimshal boundary modification was proposed by Curzon's Government on 10 August 1905. It was very small. The original 1899 proposal was that

> the line, after leaving the crest of the Mustagh range in the vicinity of the Shingshal [Shimshal] Pass, should run in an easterly direction, and then turn southwards so as just to include the part of Darwaza within the Hunza frontier. Thereafter it was to continue its southward trend until it regained the main crests.

[53] FO 539/90, No. 89, enclosing 43, Curzon to Brodrick, 10 Aug. 1905.

What Curzon now proposed was that

> the boundary should run from the Khunjerab Pass south along the main watershed, as far as a point about six miles south-west of the Oprang Pass. At this point the line should leave the main watershed, run due east for about five miles, and then continue in a south-easterly direction until it strikes the Mustagh River (incorrectly shown on maps as the Oprang) at Kuram-jilga. The Mustagh River would then form the boundary up to a point about four miles above the junction of the stream from the Shingshal Pass; from this point it would ascend the nearest high spur to the west and regain the main crest, which it would then follow on the lines indicated in Sir Claude MacDonald's despatch to the Tsungli Yamen of the 14th March 1899.[53]

This modification, which, it should be noted, in no way affected the 1899 alignment in the Aksai Chin region, brought the Mir of Hunza's territory down to the bank of the Mustagh, a tributary of the Yarkand River, and gave him some of the fertile tracts of the Raskam district.

Curzon, in 1905, also resolved upon another small modification in the 1899 proposals. When, in 1904, he suggested to the Home Government that the 1899 line be asserted unilaterally, the reply from London had contained a warning against the claiming of borders up to which the Indian Government was not in effective control. The western end of the 1899 line, it will be remembered, crossed a portion of the Taghdumbash Pamir in the upper Karachukur valley.

Here, north of the main watershed, the British did not feel themselves prepared to maintain posts, and any forces stationed there by the Mir of Hunza could be expelled without difficulty by the Chinese who had shown no signs of welcoming Hunza men across the watershed. Hence it was suggested that the new line should not cross the Karachukur; rather, it should follow the watershed around that river's sources. In effect, therefore, the new line would not start at Pavalo-Schveikhovski Peak but at a point a little bit to the south-west where the Afghan border of Wakhan left the Karachukur watershed.

These modifications, combined with the question of the Kashgar Consulate, gave rise to a proposal rather different from Curzon's original idea of a unilateral British declaration. Another note would be addressed to the Chinese, a sequel to the British note of 14 March 1899, in which the British would offer to abandon all the Hunza claims in Raskam and the Taghdumbash Pamir, provided the Chinese Government would agree to the following terms: first, the total severance of their connection with Hunza; second, the formal recognition of a frontier line which, starting from Pavalo-Schveikhovski Peak, would follow the main watershed of the Mustagh Range with the exception of the small northward projection of Hunza territory in the Shimshal region, in other words the 1905 modifications of the 1899 boundary; finally, the recognition by the Chinese of the status of Macartney as British Consul in Kashgar and the acceptance of a British Consulate in that city. In the proposed note to the Chinese emphasis was to be placed on the fact that there was contained a bargain of kinds: the Chinese would gain territory in the Taghdumbash Pamir, nominally under Hunza sovereignty of some kind, in exchange for granting Hunza absolute right over the small tracts north of the watershed beyond the Shimshal Pass.[54]

The linking of the Hunza question with that of the Kashgar Consulate was to prove unfortunate for the prospects of Anglo-Chinese boundary agreement. The India Office, in consultation with Lord Lansdowne at the Foreign Office, decided that this moment, in late 1905, was not the time to raise a matter with such far reaching implications as the location of a British Consul in Sinkiang. Negotiations were then in progress in Calcutta between the Indian Government and China over the Chinese acceptance of the Lhasa Convention which Younghusband had secured from the Tibetans in the previous year.[55] It would be most unwise to permit the two questions of Tibet and Sinkiang to become mutually involved. In 1906, after the Anglo-Chinese Convention on

[54] PSF 191/2/82, loc. cit. For modifications in the 1899 line, see Maps 13 and 17.
[55] These negotiations are discussed in detail in Lamb, *The McMahon Line*, Vol. 1, op. cit.

Tibet had been signed, the Hunza question was again raised by the Indian Government. It was now decided to separate it from the Kashgar Consulate, but to push the latter issue first. Sir John Jordan, who had succeeded Satow as British Minister in Peking, thought that the combination of Hunza and the Kashgar Consulate might prove fatal to the latter, since the Chinese had strong views on Hunza.

As Jordan reported:

I am inclined to think that there is little prospect of inducing the Chinese Government to renounce their claims over Hunza, however shadowy they may appear to be from our standpoint, in return for the concessions offered by the Indian Government. The impression which a perusal of the correspondence has left in my mind is that the occupancy rights of the Kanjutis in the Raskam Valley were never viewed with much disfavour by the Chinese, and that the abandonment of that portion of the Hunza claim would not form a valuable asset in negotiating an arrangement with the Chinese Government. On the other hand, the Central Government here [Peking] would, I think, be disposed to set considerable store by a continuance of their connection with Hunza, and I agree with Sir E. Satow's view that any proposal to renounce this connection would be very distasteful to them and be evaded as long as possible.

Jordan then went on to observe that

we know with what tenacity they [the Chinese] clung to similar claims in the cases of Corea, Burma and Tonquin, and although the tie with Kanjut is much weaker, the annual tribute forms the subject of a memorial in the Peking Gazette, and represents, with the quinquennial mission from Nepal, the only remnant of China's once extended suzerainty over distant regions on the frontiers of the Empire.

Moreover, Jordan concluded, there was extreme difficulty in 'bringing the Chinese Government to agree to any rectification of frontiers in remote districts of which they have very imperfect knowledge'. This, at any rate, had been Jordan's own experience.[56]

On Jordan's advice, accordingly, John Morley, who in late 1905 had replaced Brodrick at the India Office, told the Viceroy, Lord Minto, on 25 January 1907 that, for the time being, the project to secure the Chinese abandonment of their Hunza claims would be given up. There it lay in limbo until 1911, when two proposals were made for its revival. In that year, as a result of a Sino-Russian dispute over the terms of the 1881 St Petersburg Treaty, the Russians greatly reinforced their post at Tashkurgan—the first step, it seemed to Macartney, to the long expected Russian annexation of Kashgaria. Macartney urged that now was the time to get the border settled between British India and Sinkiang, but the Government of India, preoccupied with a Chinese problem on the frontier along the Assam Himalayas and on the Salween-

[56] PSF 1912/82, loc. cit., quoting Jordan to Grey, 13 Nov. 1906.

Irrawaddy divide in Burma, declined to create for itself difficulties in the Karakoram as well. For the same reason it had no difficulty turning down a suggestion made in October 1911 by Archibald Rose, who had lately been British Consul at Tengyueh in Yunnan, that the Chinese should be asked to hand over to the British the whole of Sarikol and the Taghdumbash Pamir in exchange for British recognition of Chinese rights at Hpimaw (Pienma) on the Burma-Yunnun frontier.[57]

In 1912, with the outbreak of the Chinese Revolution resulting in a vast increase in the size of Russian consular escorts throughout Sinkiang, the Indian Government of Lord Hardinge became most alarmed. If Russia were going to take over all of Kashgaria, which now seemed inevitable, then the British would be well advised to keep Russia as far away from the centres of population in the Indian Empire as they could. Hardinge, therefore, revived virtually without modification Sir John Ardagh's proposals of 1 January 1897.[58] The British frontier should run north of the Tagdumbash Pamir and Raskam. It should include Suget and Shahidulla. It should retain within Indian territory the whole Aksai Chin plateau. This proposal, which Hardinge made in September 1912, involved a complete abandonment of the principles of the 1899 note. The British would now claim, on behalf of Hunza, sovereignty over the Taghdumbash Pamir and Raskam; and, presumably, under British protection the Mir's subjects could cultivate across the watershed to their hearts' content. Lord Hardinge's plan was never accepted by the Home Government, nor was it rejected out of hand. It created some sort of fresh precedent for the argument that the Indian Government enjoyed a special interest in tracts along the northern slopes of the Karakoram, an argument which was reinforced in 1915, during World War I, when a British post was established beside that of the Russians at Tashkurgan. During this period, moreover, there is reason to believe that a few Hunza men began cultivating some Raskam plots with the tacit connivance of the Chinese authorities. Perhaps they had been doing this since 1908, when Macartney was at last recognised as a Consul, and when, following the signing of the Anglo-Russian Convention of 1907, tensions in Kashgar relaxed considerably.

With the easing of the Raskam problem, and with the failure of the British to force the Chinese to a formal answer

---

[57] For Rose's ideas see FO 371/1335, No. 7971 and 'The Chinese Frontiers of India', *Geographical Journal* XXXIX (1912).
[58] This boundary, which Hardinge proposed to the India Office on 12 Sept. 1912, would have followed the most extreme and northerly of the kind of alignments proposed by Ardagh, running along the Kilian Range north of Shahidulla. For the full text of Hardinge's proposal, see Lamb, *China-India Border*, op. cit., pp. 108-9, and Woodman, op. cit., pp. 79-80.

to the 1899 note, what was the status, in the eyes of the Indian Government, of the boundary alignment which Sir Claude MacDonald had indicated to the Tsungli Yamen? The basic problem which had produced its original definition, of course, remained. It still seemed likely that sooner or later the Russians would take over Kashgaria, and it would be as well to have a clearly defined border before this happened. If the British were not going to try to secure the reversionary rights to tracts north of the watershed, then the 1899 alignment was the logical boundary, especially after its sector across the Karachukur valley in the Taghdumbash Pamir had been withdrawn to the main watershed in 1905.

In 1907, perhaps as a byproduct of the negotiations then in progress in St Petersburg between Isvolski, the Russian Foreign Minister, and Sir Arthur Nicolson over Russian and British spheres of influence in various parts of Asia, the Indian Government was asked by the India Office to look into the question of its frontier alignment in the Karakoram.[59] On most British maps, of course, this line tended to follow something like the Ardagh alignment of 1897. Was this the correct boundary, Richmond Ritchie, the Secretary of the Political Department at the India Office, asked Sir Louis Dane, the Indian Foreign Secretary, in early 1907. Dane, on looking into the question, had to answer that it was not. The real boundary was not that advanced line of the old maps, though the impression that it was had not been challenged by the Indian Government which had no wish to see the Russians building roads across the northern slopes of the Karakoram towards British India. Since the 1899 offer to China the Indian Government felt that in practice the real boundary could only be that which Sir Claude MacDonald had outlined.

The weakest spot in the 1899 alignment, Dane evidently thought, was not in the Taghdumbash Pamir or Raskam, not even in the tract between the Karakoram Pass and Shahidulla, but on the Aksai Chin plateau. Here British territory did not extend right up to the Kunlun Range along the southern edge of the Tarim Basin. By the 1899 alignment the Chinese, either through Sinkiang or Tibet, had access to the plateau from which they could, in fact, outflank the Karakoram barrier; for the Aksai Chin plateau provided a series of routes all leading to the valleys of rivers flowing into the Indus. The Aksai Chin plateau, of course, also led onto the great plateau of Tibet and, in theory, it provided a route from Sinkiang to points along the entire length of the Indian

[59] The question of Sinkiang was not on the agenda of the Isvolski-Nicolson talks, though the British had at one time considered its possible inclusion. Sinkiang, however, was very much a part of the Anglo-Russian problem in Central Asia; and Macartney was to suggest that it be considered when proposals were afoot in 1915 for a revision of the entire Anglo-Russian Convention of 1907.

border in the Himalayas. It was highly undesirable, therefore, that Russia should gain a foothold on the Aksai Chin. Had not the 1899 line, in fact, created a potential foothold of this kind? Sir Louis Dane thought not. Though Sir Claude MacDonald had admitted that British territory did not cover the whole of Aksai Chin, yet he had not declared that any of the region formed part of Sinkiang. It could well be maintained that Aksai Chin was Tibetan, and that if the British border with Sinkiang did not extend to the Kunlun Range, the Tibetan border with Sinkiang did. As Dane told Ritchie on 4 July 1907, 'we hope . . . to be able to keep Aksai Chin in Tibet in order to adhere to a Kuenlun boundary for that country as far as possible'. Tibet, in 1907, was about to become a rather good buffer against Russia. By the Anglo-Russian Convention, which was signed in St Petersburg a few weeks after Dane wrote these words, the Russians agreed not to make any political penetration into Tibet. Thus, without having to take any direct responsibility for the desolate Aksai Chin waste, the British had the treaty right to keep the Russians out of it. Accordingly, the Indian Foreign Department showed the 1899 alignment as the British border on a map they included in the 1909 edition of Aitchison's *Collection of Treaties*, and the Intelligence Division of the War Office in London, once the home of Sir John Ardagh, showed it on a map of Sinkiang which they brought out in 1908.

As a result of the 1912 crisis in Sinkiang, when the prospect of Russian annexation following the outbreak of the Chinese Revolution led Lord Hardinge to revive for a moment the Ardagh boundary of 1897, the Indian Government resolved to take the next favourable opportunity to make sure that the Aksai Chin was Tibetan rather than Chinese. The opportunity came with the Simla Conference of 1913-14, when British, Chinese and Tibetan representatives met to discuss the status and limits of Tibet following the collapse of Chinese power in Lhasa in 1912. The Simla Conference is outside our present scope.[60] It is worth noting, however, that the document to which it gave rise, the so called Simla Convention, did contain a veiled reference to the problem of the Aksai Chin plateau. The Simla Convention appeared in two versions. One text was initialled by the British, Chinese, and Tibetan delegates on 27 April 1914. Another, slightly modified text, the April text having been repudiated by the Chinese Government, was initialled by the British and Tibetan delegates on 3 July 1914, and confirmed by a declaration signed by the two parties that they would consider the Convention to be binding pending eventual Chinese signature. Attached to both versions of the Simla Convention was a fairly small scale map, a little less than 1:4,000,000, on

---

[60] For a detailed account of the Simla Conference of 1913-14 see Lamb, *The McMahon Line*, Vol. 2, op. cit.

which were marked the boundaries between Inner and Outer Tibet, that is to say between the territory of the Dalai Lama and that part of Tibet which was under Chinese control. There were two lines on this map. One, in red, marked the limits of the whole area understood by the term 'Tibet'. While in the main confined to indicating the border between China and Tibet, this red line also showed a stretch of border between Tibet and British India along the Assam Himalayas, which has since achieved fame as the 'McMahon Line' and to which many international lawyers attach great significance. A second line on the Simla Convention map was in blue. This marked the division between Inner and Outer Tibet. The map with these two lines was initialled by the British, Chinese, and Tibetan delegates on 27 April 1914. It was signed and sealed by the British and Tibetan delegates on 3 July 1914, following the Chinese repudiation of the Simla proceedings.

The red line on the Simla Convention map, the eastern or right hand extremity of which was the McMahon Line, extended westwards to a point roughly on the 79th meridian of east longitude. Here, for about a degree, the red line followed a course to all intents and purposes that which the present border claimed by India follows in the Aksai Chin area, a line north of the border indicated in the 1899 proposals. The implications of this part of the red line are clear enough. The territory south of it, down to the 1899 line, was Tibetan, not Chinese. In the Simla Convention map, therefore, we possess strong evidence that the securing of a Tibetan Aksai Chin, advocated in 1907 by Sir Louis Dane, was carried out by Sir Henry McMahon. The Aksai Chin portion of the red line has just as much validity in international law as the McMahon Line portion. The Indian Government today, which has placed great stress on the McMahon Line portion of this particular map, has probably committed itself, albeit unknowingly, to a Tibetan Aksai Chin. It could even be argued that the Aksai Chin portion of the red line, reinforced as it is by the 1899 note, possesses greater force in international law than the McMahon Line portion, the latter embodying an essentially novel boundary alignment.[61]

For our present purposes it suffices to observe that the Simla Convention map is evidence that Hardinge's revival in 1912 of the Ardagh boundary had no lasting effect, and that by 1914 the British had again reverted to a more moderate position, at least in the Aksai Chin area; from it we may perhaps conclude that the 1899 line had managed to survive the crisis of the outbreak of the Chinese Revolution in Sinkiang.

[61] For the Simla Convention map and its implications in the Aksai Chin region, see Maps 9 and 10.

# Postscript

The story of the Raskam problem and the origins of the 1899 line contained here very strongly suggests that, by 1907, the Government of India really knew that, if it were obliged to define formally a boundary in the Aksai Chin region, it would have to follow something like the 1899 line proposed by Sir Claude MacDonald to the Chinese rather than the kind of line which Sir John Ardagh was advocating in 1897. This conclusion is reinforced by the implications of the map appended to the Simla Convention of 1914, which indicated that the Kunlun crest line divided Tibet from Sinkiang in the Aksai Chin region and not British India from Sinkiang. Yet, as we have seen, in the 1950s the Government of India, the successor to the British Raj, was still claiming a border in this region which owed something to Ardagh and which quite ignored the implications of the 1899 note. Why was this?[1]

The answer to this question has yet to be solved adequately

---

[1] It certainly should be noted that by the early 1950s a great deal of cartographic uncertainty existed as to where the northern and northeastern boundaries of Ladakh might be. Map 8, which compares important maps of 1874, 1947, and 1950, shows a surprisingly wide range of alignments with the U.S. Air Force disagreeing radically on this question with the U.S. Army. It is undoubtedly possible that, faced with such public confusion, the Government of India felt itself free to select the line which best suited its purposes. This possibility, however, in no way reduces the significance of the 1899 line as modified in 1905.

by scholars. During the last years of British rule in India it was the practice of official British cartography to show no boundary at all in the Aksai Chin area and along the Karakoram. Even the published (1947) diary of K. P. S. Menon, who was to become a senior diplomat in the service of the Government of Independent India, had as its dust jacket a section of a map of these mountainous tracts with the words 'Boundary Undefined' marking that region which was soon to be the subject of such acrimonious Sino-Indian argument.[2] In 1954, however, the Government of India did produce an official map which showed a line of boundary for Ladakh.[3] This line is interesting because it is a peculiar mixture of Ardagh and the 1899 proposals. In the western part, that is to say along the portions of the Karakoram which were by then under effective Pakistani control, it showed a line which more or less followed the Karakoram crests and which gave to China a great deal of territory which Ardagh would certainly have argued ought to remain within the Indian sphere. In the Aksai Chin, however, it showed a line far north of the 1899 proposals and strongly reminiscent of the *Kashmir Atlas* of 1868. It is a further odd feature of this particular map that it also claimed along the Ladakh-Tibet border in the Panggong Lake region and at the Indus crossing some small tracts which the British, so the available cartographical evidence would suggest, had *never* claimed.[4] Where did this 1954 Indian boundary come from and why was it raised at this particular moment in time? We can here but advance a number of hypotheses which may possibly, for all their uncertainty, be of some interest.

The first hypothesis is that the 1954 Indian map owed much to the files of the Indian External Affairs Department going back to British days. For much of the 1930s and, indeed, up to 1942, Sinkiang was dominated by the warlord Sheng Shih-t'sai who was thought by many British observers to be a Russian puppet.[5] During this time, which also was a period when Indian diplomacy was supervised by Sir Olaf Caroe, there can be no doubt that Soviet influence in Sinkiang was present and that it was potentially as likely to lead to Russian annexation (even if in the veiled manner applied in Outer Mongolia) as it had ever been in the days when George

---

[2]K. P. S. Menon, *Delhi-Chungking, a travel diary*, London 1947.
[3]On the question of Indian maps since 1947, indeed on all stages of the modern evolution of the Sino-Indian boundary question, see Maxwell, op. cit.
[4]See Map 20. It is outside our present scope, though it is fascinating to observe the steady advance of British ideas about the northern and northeastern frontiers of the State of Jammu and Kashmir between 1846, when the State really came into being under British paramountcy, and 1895 when the story in Paper I opens. For British ideas about the Ladakh-Tibet border *c.* 1846, see Map 18.
[5]For a slightly more detailed discussion of British attitudes towards Sinkiang in the 1930s, see Lamb, *Asian Frontiers*, op. cit., pp. 102-4.

Macartney was combating Petrovski in Kashgar. It is probable that during these years the Indian Foreign Department started laying the groundwork for an Ardagh pattern boundary for just the kind of reasons which Sir John Ardagh had so lucidly stated in his paper of 1 January 1897. Such preparation, of course, did not of necessity involve too clear an explanation of its thoughts by the Government of India to the India Office in London. In order to know quite what was happening, therefore, one would have to see not only the London records, but also the files preserved in New Delhi, and these are for this period closed to all but the most loyal supporters of modern Indian policy. The present author, at any rate, is hardly likely to be allowed to see them in the foreseeable future. There do exist, however, one or two odd facts which may perhaps be symptomatic of the general trend.

First, it is certain that in the late 1930s the Indian Government was very much concerned at the growing threat of Russian influence in Sinkiang, a threat which of course also involved by extension the whole question of the security of Tibet and the long Himalayan border, The present author was told by the late Sir Michael Gillett, at this time serving in the British Consulate in Kashgar, that in either 1937 or 1938 there were actually minor armed clashes between Chinese and British patrols along the Karakoram in the Hunza region. One consequence of this situation was the British decision to terminate once and for all, all signs and symbols of any tributary relationship to China on the part of the Mir of Hunza. The Mir, so it is said, was somewhat upset by the cancellation of what at first sight would have seemed the fiscal burden of paying tribute to the Chinese. His dislike of this move was caused by two main factors. In the first place, his tribute to the Chinese in Sinkiang was really nominal in cash terms and he received in gifts from the Chinese authorities far more than he paid out in tribute. In the second place, Hunza cultivation across the Karakoram watershed, particularly in the Shimshal area, was immediately put in jeopardy. In this connection it is interesting to observe that in the Sino-Pakistani boundary agreement of 1963 the Chinese conceded to Pakistan a by no means insignificant tract here, no doubt to help meet Hunza requirements.

Second, we know that the Tibetan implications of the growing Soviet presence in Sinkiang caused the Indian Foreign Department under Sir Olaf Caroe to think again about doing something about the McMahon Line border in the Assam Himalayas, a border which had between 1914 and 1936 been almost completely forgotten in New Delhi. It has been shown by John Addis and Neville Maxwell, among others, that at this time the Indian Government revised Volume 14 of the 1929 edition of Aitchison's collection of treaties so as to create the impression that the Simla Convention of 1914 had a great deal more force in international law than it in fact did. The original version of Volume 14 of Aitchison (1929 edition) stated that the Simla Conference failed to produce, because of Chinese refusal to sign, any binding agreement; it did not print the text of the secret Anglo-Tibetan notes of March 1914 which are the real basis for the McMahon Line border alignment. The revised version of the volume, while still bearing the date 1929, printed the text of these notes and gave a quite different impression, namely that the Simla proceedings had a legally binding import. Librarians in a variety of institutions, including the British Foreign Office, were asked in 1937 to replace the original version with the revised volume.[6] If this kind of sleight of hand was going on in the case of the McMahon Line, at that time but indirectly threatened by the Sinkiang situation, one may well wonder what was being done vis-à-vis the Aksai Chin and the Karakoram. One should add, however, that if any unilateral modification of boundary lines by the Government of India took place at this period, those responsible were acting out of motives of impeccable patriotism. The only regret is that if they did so act, then they created most troublesome legacy for their successors, the Government of independent India. It might have been better if they had left well enough alone and adhered to the decision to accept the 1899 line as the effective British frontier, a decision which we have noted both the Government of India and the India Office admitted in 1907 and which, albeit obliquely, the Government of India reiterated in 1914 in the map appended to the abortive Simla Convention.

Let us assume, at any rate, that the Ladakh boundary published by the Indian Government in 1954 was an imperial legacy, and let us examine briefly some of the main implications of that legacy. Two points are of prime importance. First, by some irony of fate the Aksai Chin, than which no territory in the period of British rule could have seemed to possess less practical value, turned out to be the easiest—perhaps, indeed, the only—route for an all-seasons motor road which could link Western Sinkiang with Western Tibet. As such, it naturally became a focal point in Chinese strategic thinking once the Chinese were faced with challenges to their control over both these regions and particularly Tibet. The

---

[6]John Addis discussed this matter at some length in his *The India-China Border Question*, privately circulated by the Centre for International Affairs, Harvard University, in Feb. 1963. I was permitted to refer to this work in *The McMahon Line*, op. cit. Vol. 2, p. 546, n. 26. More recently Maxwell, op. cit., p. 55, has also gone into this fascinating episode. See also K. Gupta, 'The McMahon Line', op. cit., for a full discussion of the whole question of the 1938 revision of Vol. XIV of Aitchison's *Treaties* on the basis of the records of the India Office which have recently been opened to public inspection.

Chinese Communists occupied (or, as they would have put it, reoccupied or liberated) Tibet in 1950, and between that date and the outbreak of the great Tibetan revolt in 1959 their position on the roof of the world was definitely uneasy. In these circumstances they could not contemplate what the Indians were demanding of them, namely the abandonment of their major route into the western extremity of Tibet. Second, by yet another irony of fate, this very same Aksai Chin formed part of Ladakh (at least in Indian eyes after the publication of the 1954 maps); and Ladakh was a district of the State of Jammu and Kashmir, the possession of which India had been actively disputing with Pakistan ever since October 1947. Any Indian surrender of Kashmiri territory to any foreign power would of course be a most unfortunate precedent highly detrimental to the arguments which India was then raising in support of her claims and would provide potential ammunition for her Pakistani opponents.[7]

The essential point in the considerations just noted is simple. Aksai Chin became in the 1950s something far more than a rather academic bone of Sino-Indian contention of verbal import only. Implicit in the Aksai Chin question were factors which concerned vitally the internal attitudes and policies of both China and India, and neither power could

[7]The author has commented on this point in a review of Maxwell, *India's China War*, in *Modern Asian Studies* V, 4 (1971), pp. 389-97.

afford to make concessions. Initially, the Chinese were in the most favourable position because soon after they began their attack on Tibet in 1950 they were in physical control of the region, and they have in this sense had an advantage over the Indians ever since. Once India, however, made a formal claim to Aksai Chin, as took place with the publication of Indian maps in 1954, possession by China might have been nine points of the law but the tenth point sufficed to complicate gravely the pattern of Chinese international relations. Assuming that China does not contemplate the physical conquest of India, one suspects that the only practicable theoretical solution of the Aksai Chin question lies in an Indian gesture following a satisfactory Indian solution of the Kashmir problem, and it is hard to see such a solution as implying anything much less than the destruction of the State of Pakistan as a sovereign entity.

Up to 1959 Pakistan, as well as Kashmiri nationalists who sought independence from both India and Pakistan, saw the Aksai Chin question in a similar light. There were moments, indeed, as during Chou En-lai's Indian visit in 1956, when Pakistani statesmen, anticipating a possible Sino-Indian border agreement, warned India not to give away Kashmiri territory in the Aksai Chin area of Ladakh. After 1959, however, the Pakistanis, always in Kashmir essentially on the psychological defensive, began their journey along the road to rapprochement with Peking. In the process they abandoned not only Aksai Chin, which in any case lay well beyond their practical grasp, but also all other extreme Ardagh-type claims north of the main Karakoram watershed. In this frame of mind they were able without too much difficulty to come to a border agreement with China in March 1963 which was little more than a confirmation of the western part of the 1899 line as it was unilaterally modified by Lord Curzon's Government of India in 1905. Thus the 1899 line, the ignoring of which contributed so much to Sino-Indian hostility, made a more positive contribution to international relations as, by its implicit acceptance, one of the foundations of Sino-Pakistani friendship.

This is not the place to expand further on the potentialities latent in the present unhappy state of international relations on the Indian subcontinent. Our main subjects, after all, are the 1899 boundary proposals in Ladakh and points (which might at first sight seem rather abstruse) relating to the Mir of Hunza's interests to the north of the main Karakoram watershed at the turn of the nineteenth and twentieth centuries. One must conclude, however, with the observation that these matters had by 1907 induced the British Government of India to adopt a boundary policy towards Ladakh and the Karakoram which, had it been adhered to in later days, would have saved India, China, and Pakistan a great deal of pain and suffering and the rest of the world much trouble and concern.

# Maps

*Maps 1 and 2* are designed merely to provide some general geographical setting for the area covered by the two papers reproduced in this work. Map 1 shows a boundary for the north-eastern corner of Ladakh which is really a compromise between Chinese and Indian claims. I have put the eastern boundary of Tibet with China far more to the west than is often the case in even the most modern atlases—what I have tried to indicate here is the effective eastern limit of direct Lhasa administration as of about 1900 A.D. In Map 2 no boundaries of any sort are indicated between Sinkiang, India, and Tibet, though I have shown boundaries between Sinkiang and Russia (including the undemarcated stretch in the Sarikol range) and also the boundaries of the Wakhan district of Afghanistan.

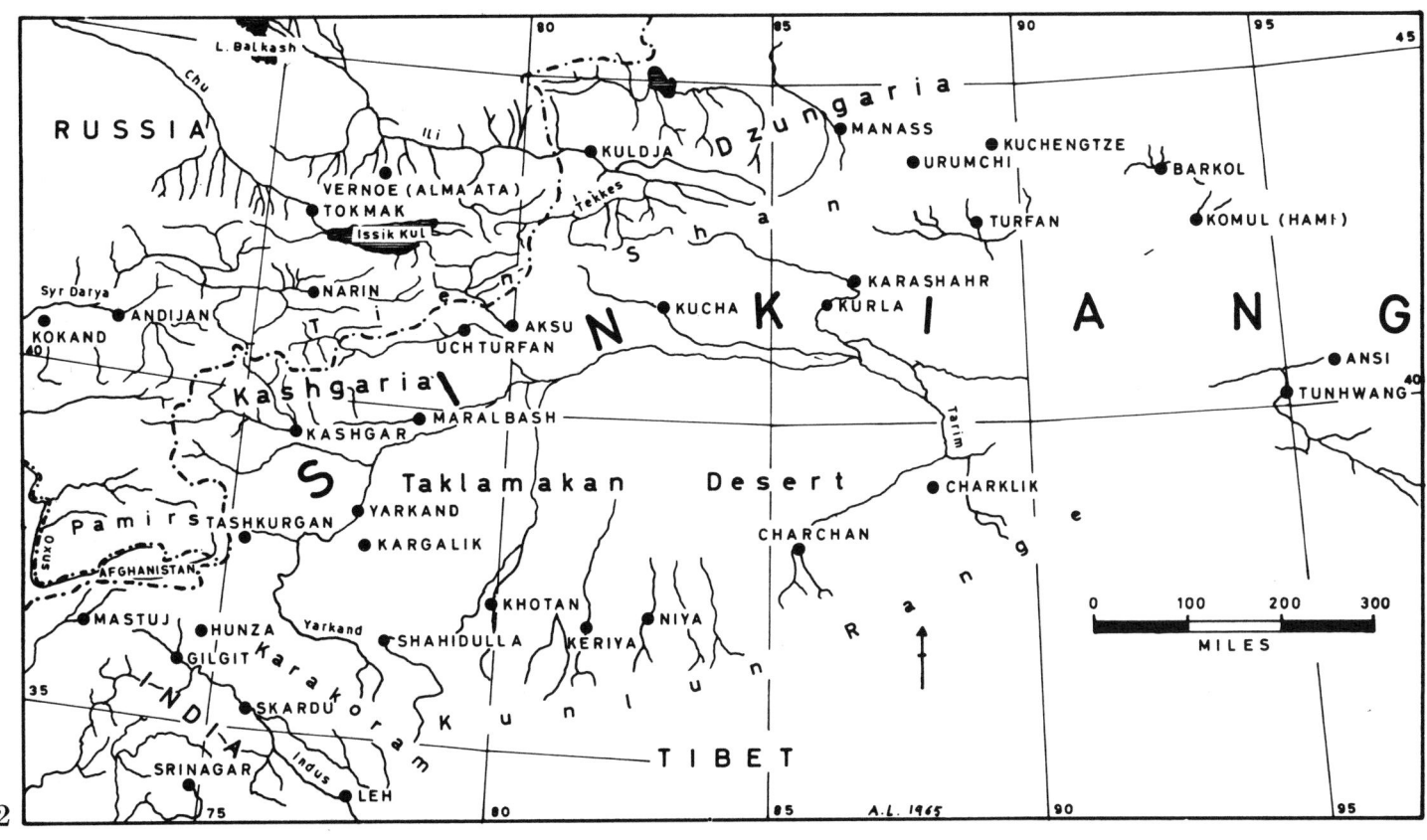

*Map 1: Sinkiang and its neighbours*

*Map 2: Sinkiang showing principal towns*

*Map 3* is intended to provide the reader with a rapid picture of the general relationship of the Chinese road in the Aksai Chin to both the 1899 line and the present border claimed by India.

Map 3: *The western sector of the Sino-Indian boundary dispute, showing the relationship of the 1899 line to the modern Chinese roads and the present Indian-claimed border with Chinese territory in Tibet and Sinkiang*

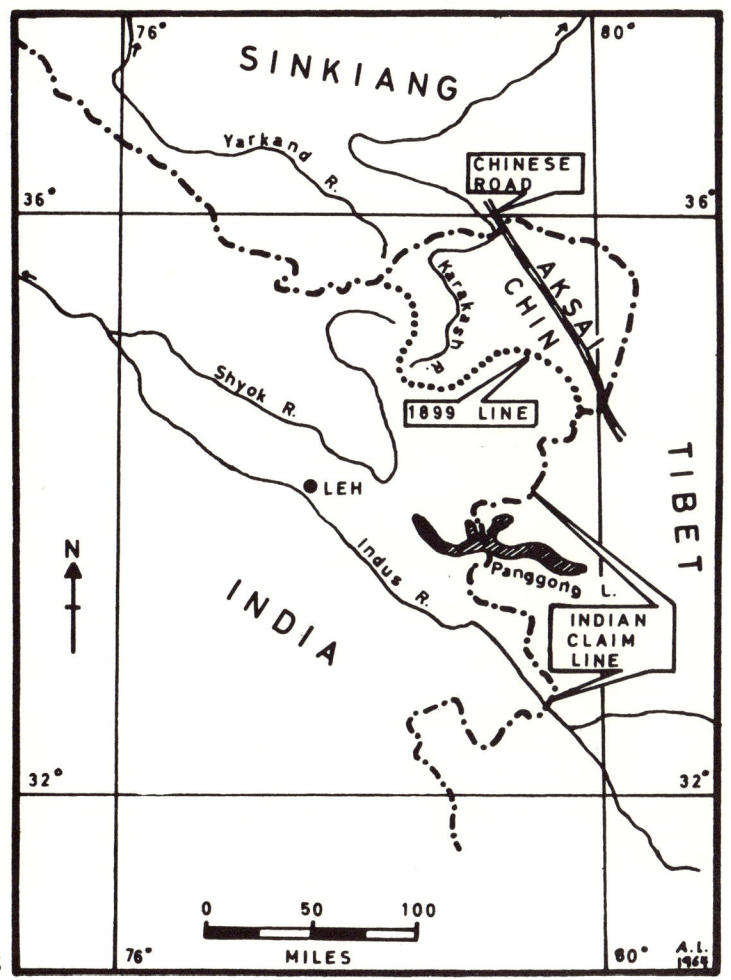

*Maps 4, 5, and 6* are designed to indicate the major watershed systems in the Pamirs, Karakoram, the western Kunlun, and the Aksai Chin and Lingzitang plateaus as a general geographical frame of reference for the understanding of boundary arguments based on the watershed principle.[1] Taking all three maps together, one cannot fail to see how the line from the Hindu Kush through the Karakoram to the range dividing the Shyok tributary of the Indus from the Karakash flowing from the Aksai Chin plateau into the Tarim basin constitutes a natural watershed line far more convenient for boundary purposes than any line involving the Kunlun mountains, which have their western terminus well on the Tarim side of the main waterpartings.[2]

[1] Geographers apparently prefer nowadays the term 'waterparting' rather than 'watershed'. I have adhered to watershed mainly because it is a word which figures so prominently in recent Sino-Indian diplomatic exchanges.
[2] Map 6 shows the Loqzung (or Lak Tsung) range referred to in the 1899 note. Some Indians, and their apologists, have in recent years denied that this range exists. It is true that the mountains here are rather less dramatic than elsewhere in the Karakoram and Kunlun; but a study of the excellent photographs taken from the Gemini satellite program and made available by NASA leaves one in no doubt that a range of sorts exists here and could be identified easily enough on the ground.

*Map 4: Major watersheds in the Pamirs and the western end of the Karakoram*

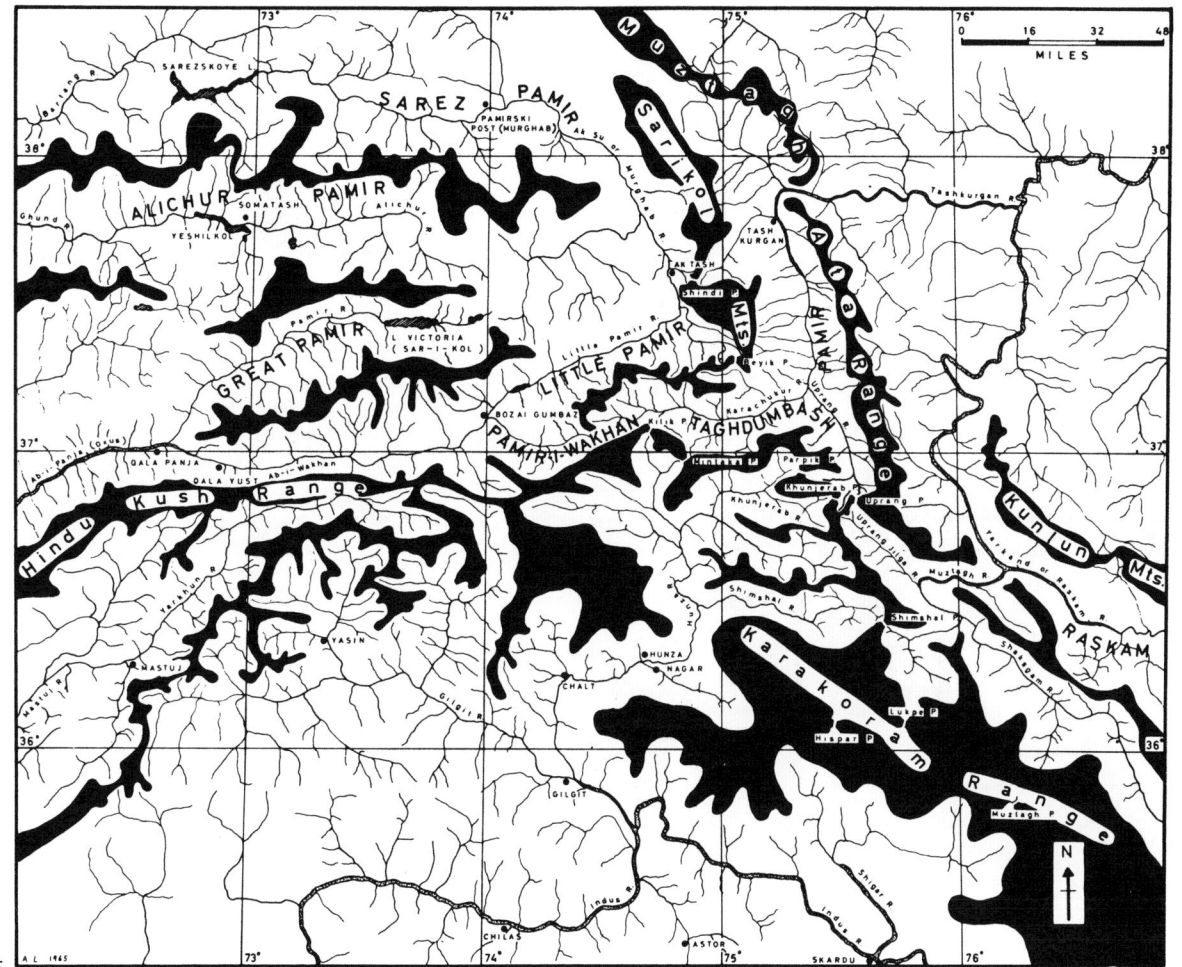

4

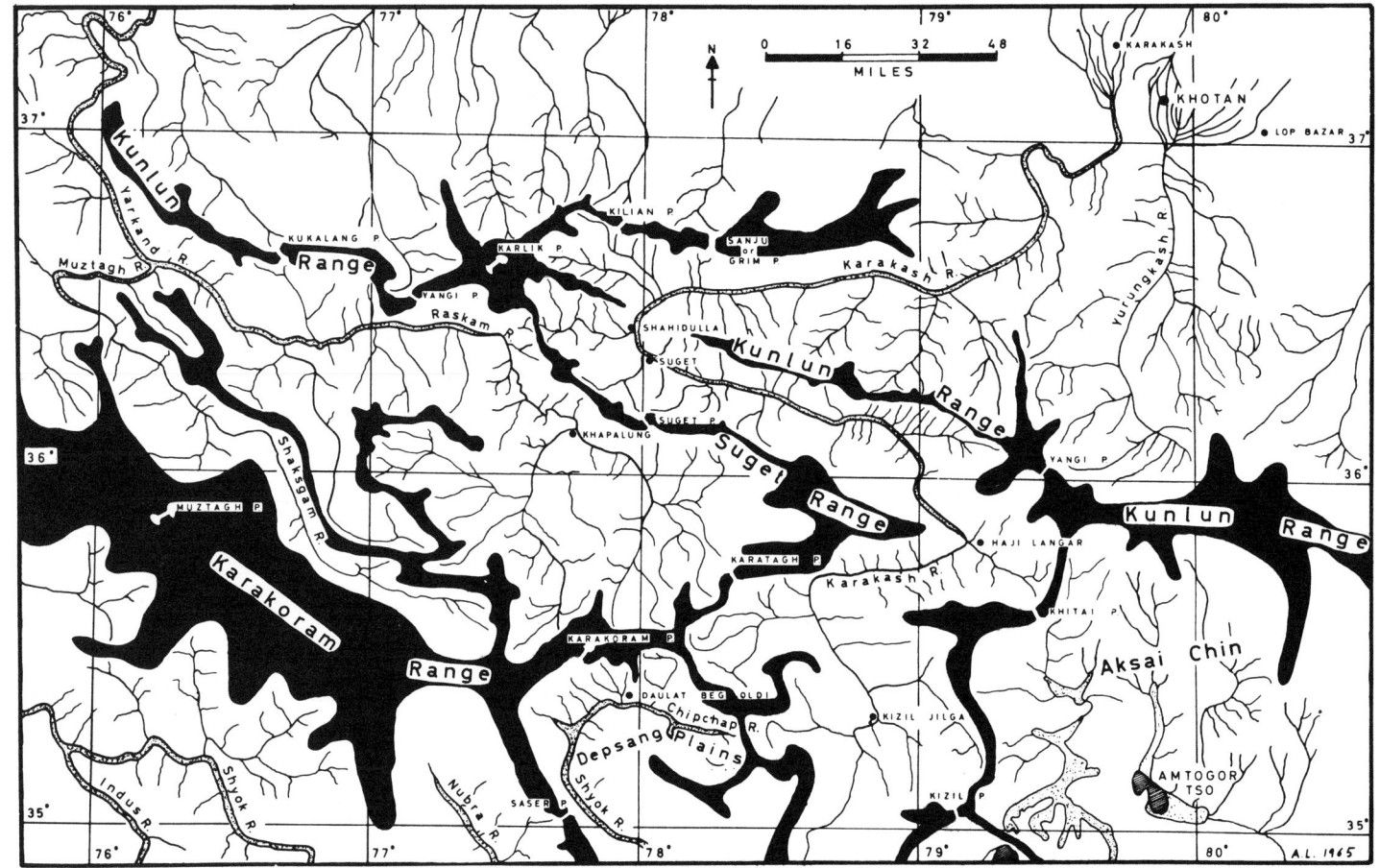

*Map 5: Major watersheds in the eastern Karakoram and the western Kunlun*
*Map 6: Major watersheds in the Aksai Chin and Lingzitang plateaus*

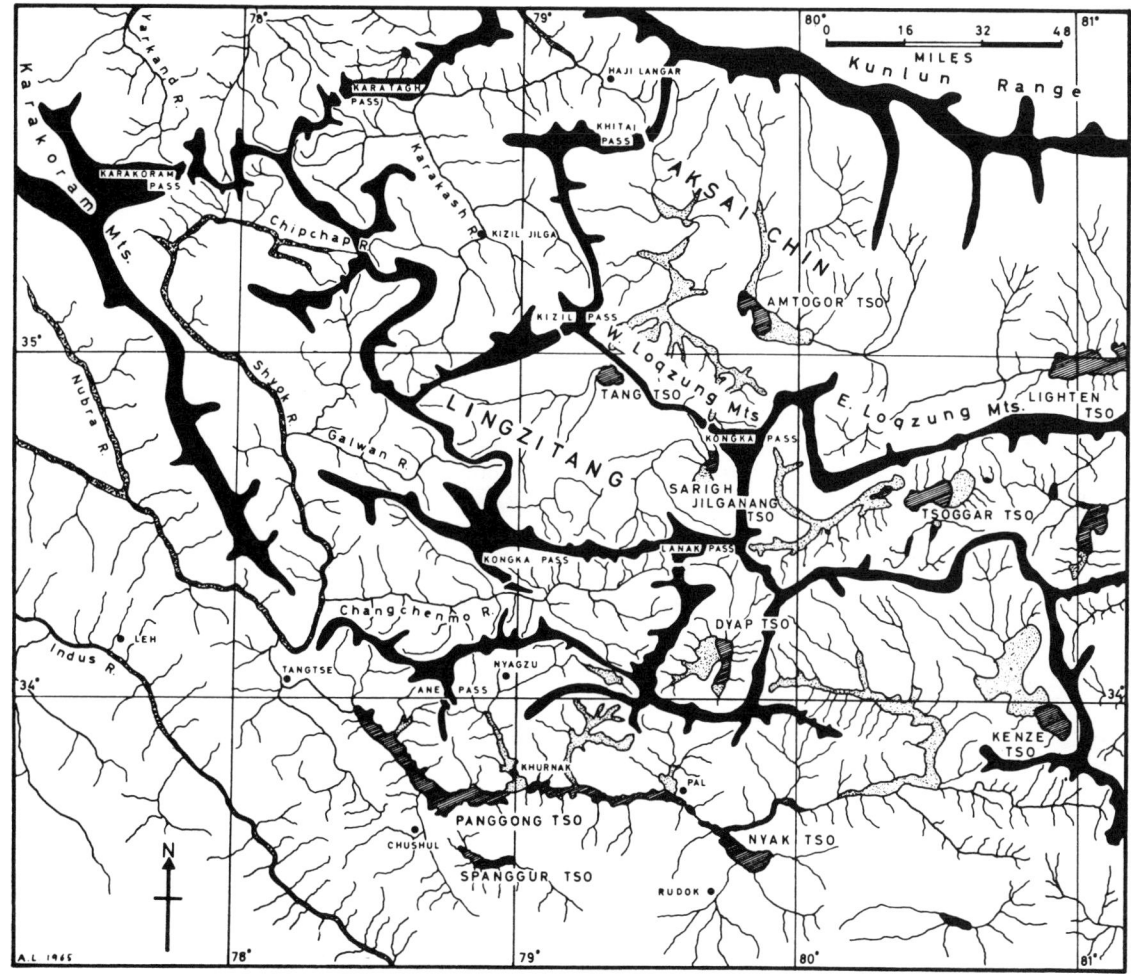

*Map 7* consists of two maps placed side by side, Map A on the left and Map B on the right. Map A is based on tracings from the *Kashmir Atlas* of 1868 and Drew's map of 1874 as well as on other sources of late nineteenth century date. The key point here, indicated by the black arrow, is the way in which the streams flowing into the Sarigh Jilganang Lake appear to rise well to the east of the 80th meridian, a feature which owes its origin to the survey work of Johnson in the 1860s. Johnson was plane tabling and he assumed that the highest peaks he could see to his east as he passed northwards across the desolation of Lingzitang and Aksai Chin on his way to Khotan constituted points on the watershed line. This was an assumption frequently made by Indian surveyors until far into the twentieth century; and it often resulted in major errors. Whole glacier systems and internal basins were overlooked. In the case of the eastern edge of the Lingzitang-Aksai Chin region, at all events, subsequent survey work, much of it carried out by members of Sven Hedin's Sino-Swedish expedition between the two World Wars, showed that the drainage system of the Sarigh Jilganang Lake did not extend east of the 80th meridian. On the right hand map, B, the eastern terminus of the Sarigh Jilganang drainage basin is indicated by a black arrow marked 1. This was clearly the point which the proposers of the 1899 line had in mind for its eastern end. If one takes the verbal expression of that line, however, without reference to cartographical progress since the 1890s, it could be argued that the line should end at the point indicated by the black arrow marked 2. To accept this, of course, would involve the abandonment here of the watershed principle and India has always maintained that her northern border is a watershed alignment. It has been over this question of interpretation that Dr S. Gopal and others have based their quarrel with my interpretation of the 1899 line. The point, of course, is that if it really did extend to the point indicated by the arrow marked 2 on Map B, then it would indeed just cut across the trace of the Chinese Sinkiang-Tibet motor road; and, hence, the Chinese would be shown to have been guilty of aggression even if the 1899 line were proved to be the true border. By the 1960s it would seem that a large vested interest existed in the maintenance of the validity of the charge that China was an aggressor vis-à-vis India. This is, of course, really a micropoint; and if the 1899 line were accepted even with the 1899 geographical co-ordinates unchanged, then in realistic Sino-Indian negotiations the whole matter could be cleared up by the Chinese agreeing to a small detour of a few miles in the trace of their road. But if the 1899 co-ordinates were to be accepted, it must be admitted that it would be no easy task to establish the point shown by the black arrow marked 2 on the actual ground. Maps of this region still are far from perfect. Perhaps a joint boundary commission provided with the admirable American photographs taken from satellites (or, for that matter, unpublished Russian photographs which no doubt also exist) could settle things once and for all. It is interesting in this context to note that in the Sino-Pakistani discussions leading up to the border agreement of March 1963 it was necessary to execute a joint survey to reconcile discrepancies between Pakistani and Chinese maps which, if taken at their face value, would have involved more than 200 square miles of territory.

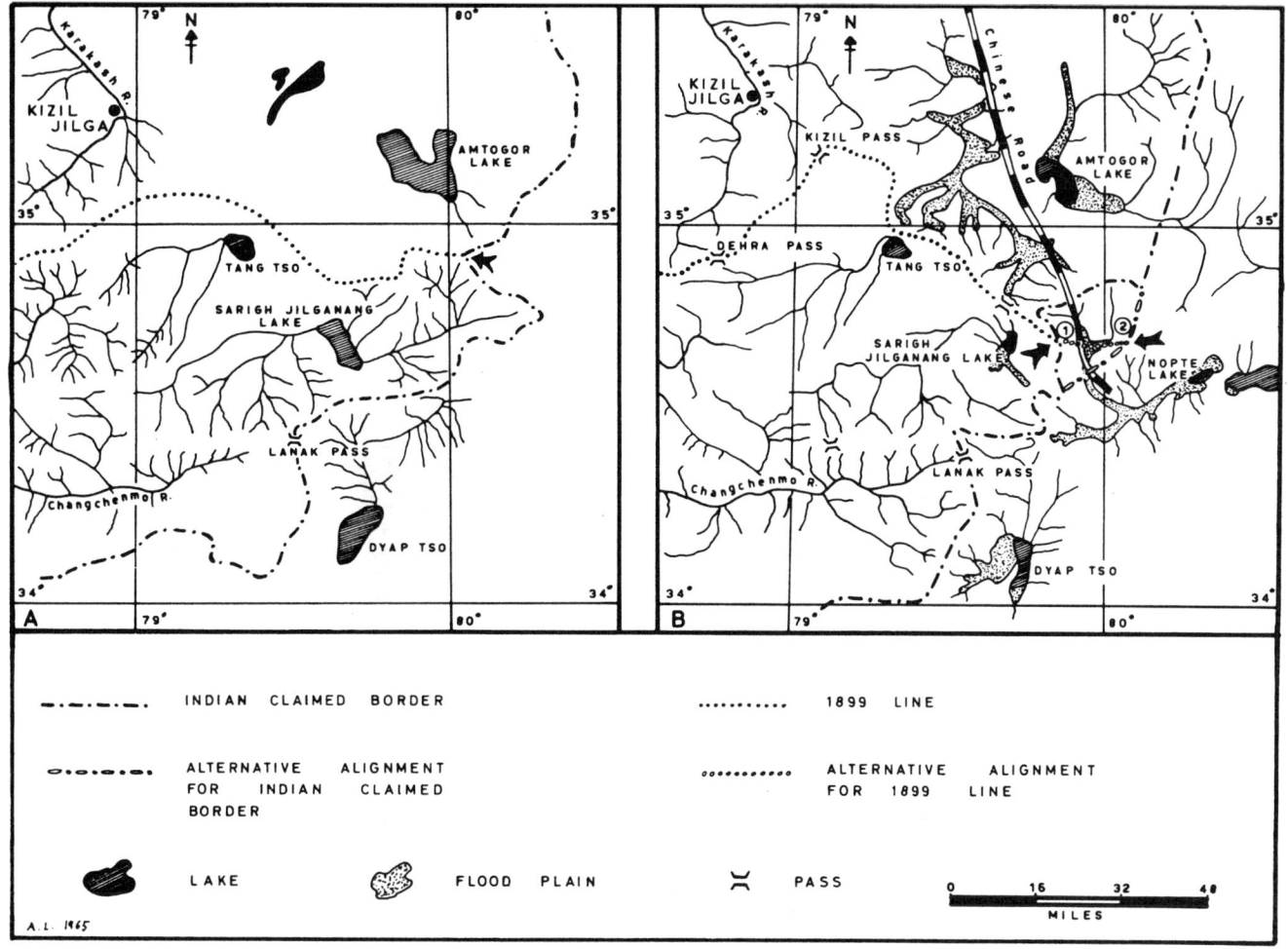

*Map 7: The Aksai Chin and the plotting of the 1899 line: comparison between old and new maps*

*Map 8* illustrates the point about cartographical deficiencies mentioned above. Here I have overlaid tracings from three maps, that of Drew (working on behalf of the Kashmir Durbar in 1874) and two maps of American origin, one issued by the U.S. Army and one by the U.S. Air Force. It will be seen that at the point indicated by the two black arrows, the crucial eastern terminus of the 1899 line, none of the maps agrees with another. It is interesting that the U.S. Air Force seems to have adopted a version of the 1899 boundary though carrying it eastwards, in total disregard for watersheds, to the point shown on such archaic maps as the *Kashmir Atlas* of 1868, while the U.S. Army has stuck to the watersheds as they were known by 1950. The U.S. Army, however, at the northern end of its boundary line as shown here, is already zooming away from the Indian-claimed border into some variety of the Ardagh-proposed alignment. It would be fascinating to see what Chinese military maps, the Communist ones no doubt derived from their Republican predecessors and based to a great extent on the work of Sven Hedin's Sino-Swedish surveyors, have to show on this point. It has always seemed to me that the Chinese military engineers in the field who were actually charged with the task of the construction of the Sinkiang-Tibet road in the 1950s had at their disposal maps which left them in no doubt that they were working on their own side of the border.

*Map 8: Borders in the Aksai Chin area: a comparison of alignments from maps published in 1874, 1947 and 1950*

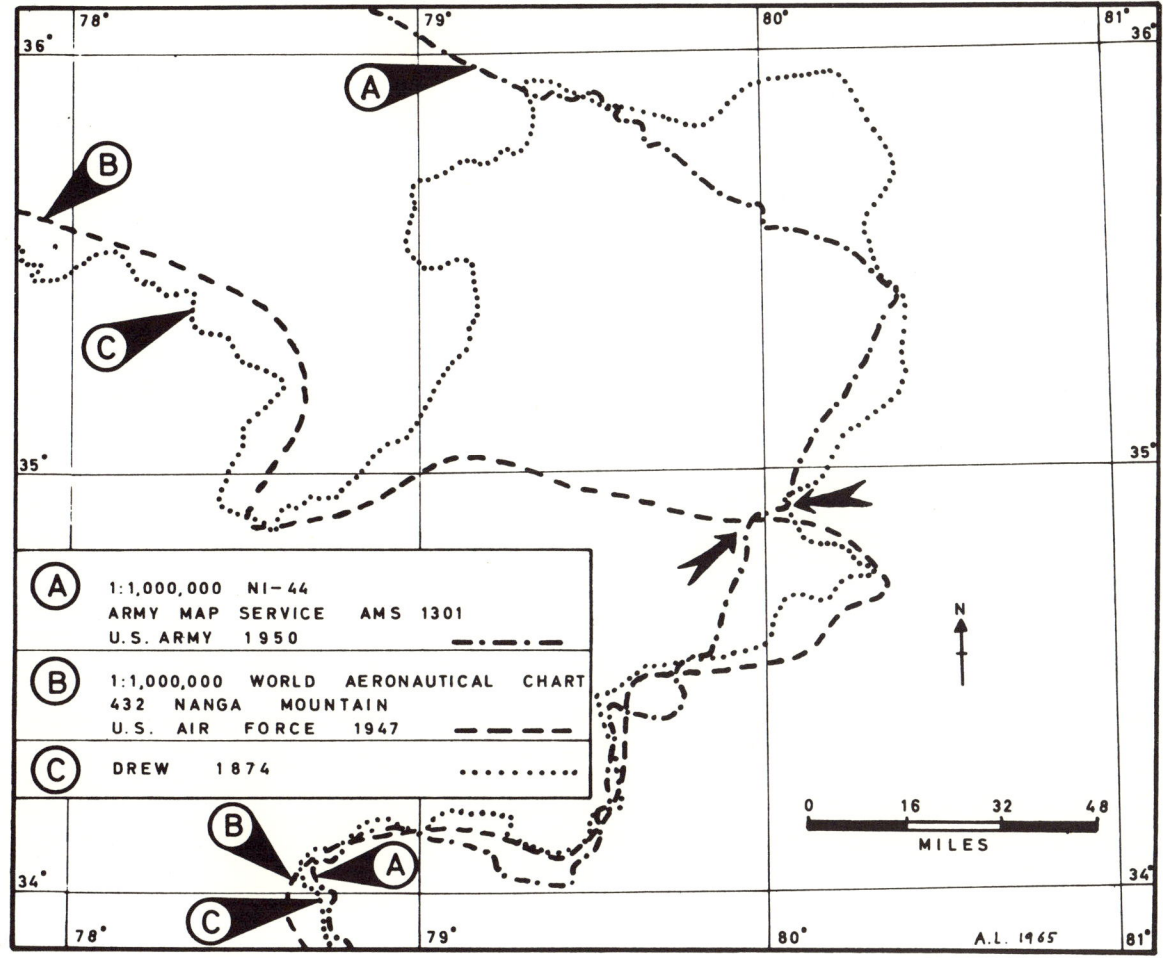

*Map 9* is a slightly simplified trace of the map appended to both texts of the Simla Convention of 1914 (a subject which I have discussed at length in Volume 2 of *The McMahon Line*). This map carries the initials of the Chinese delegate at the conference, Chen I-fan, who was under the impression that it concerned solely the borders between Inner and Outer Tibet and Outer Tibet and China. He certainly did not regard it as in any way being a definition of the Sino-Indian border, as has since been argued, though in fact the bottom right hand extremity of the red line is actually the famous McMahon Line between Assam in British India and Tibet. Our present concern here is rather with the top left hand extremity of the red line, which explicitly separates Inner Tibet from China (in this region Sinkiang).

*Map 9: A slightly simplified tracing of the map appended to the Simla Convention of 1914 and showing boundaries of Inner and Outer Tibet*

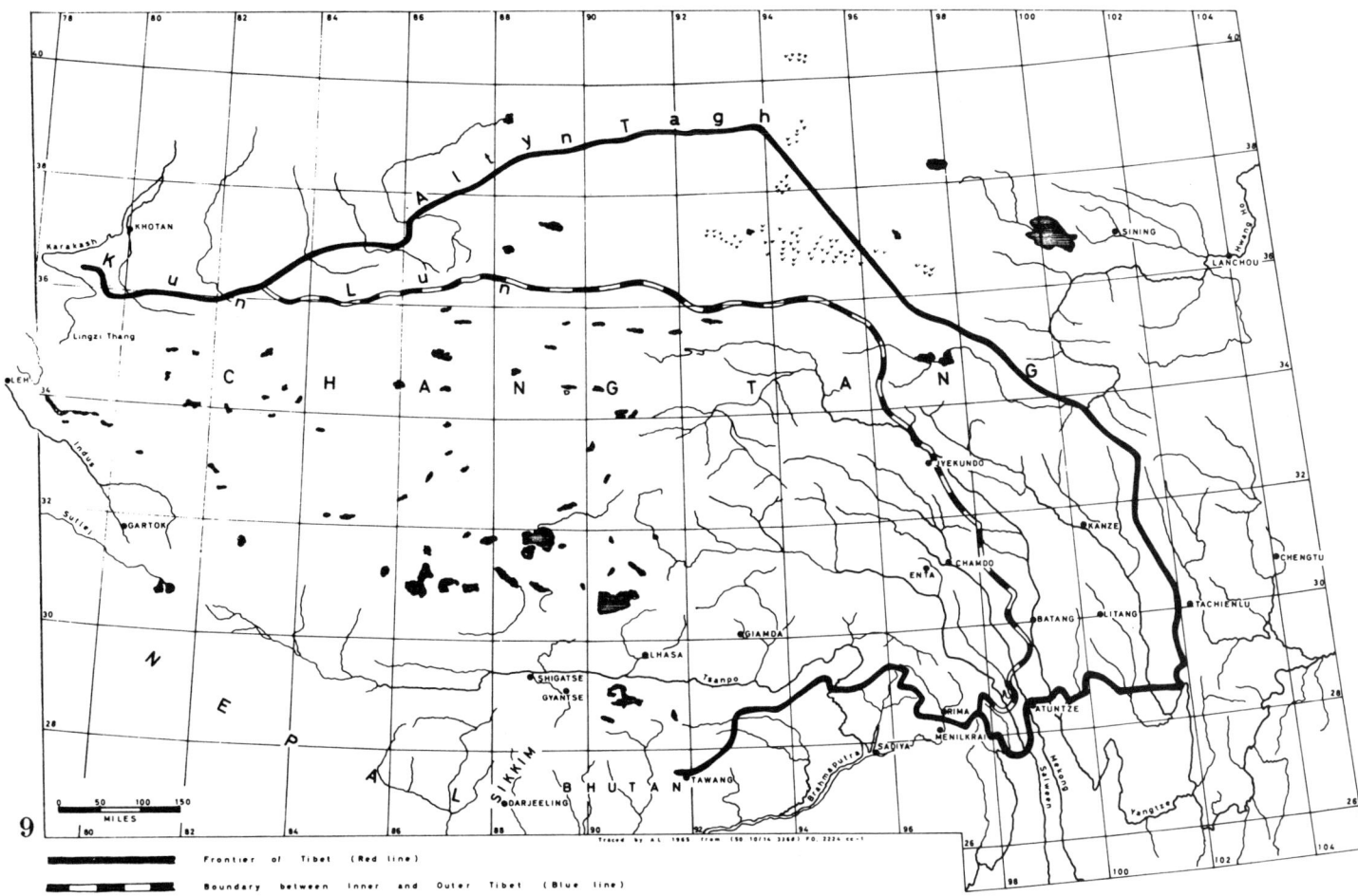

*Map 10* is a detailed exposition of the point just made above. The left hand extremity, separating Inner Tibet from Sinkiang in the Simla Convention map, follows precisely the same course in the stretch marked A on the left hand map as does the Indian claimed Sino-Indian border on the right hand map, and it is hard to see how this line can indicate anything but a border between Inner Tibet and Sinkiang. The failure of scholars for so long to notice this point, despite the vast corpus of literature generated by the Sino-Indian boundary question, is indication enough of the rather casual approach adopted by some writers who have expressed strong views on the rights and wrongs of the matter.

*Map 10: Comparison between the extreme north-western end of the red line in the 1914 Simla Convention map and the present Indian claim line in Ladakh along the Kunlun range*

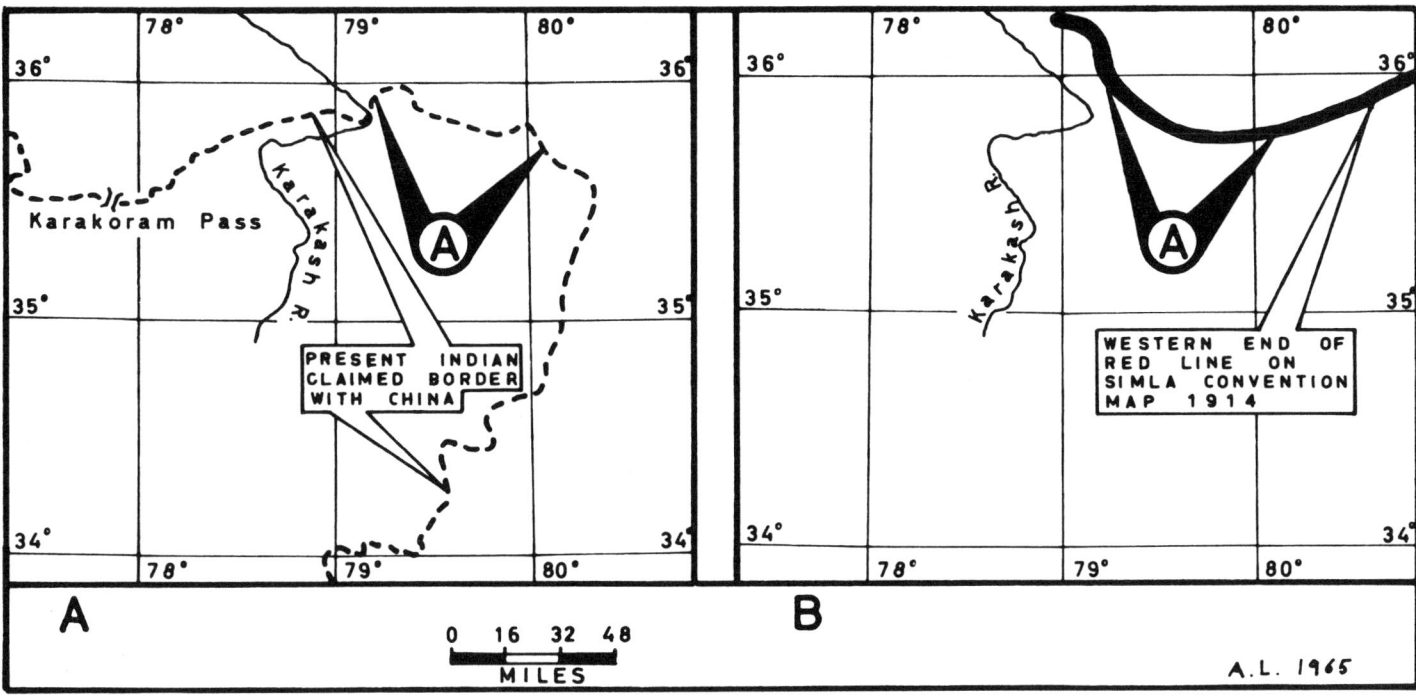

*Map 11* shows my reconstruction of the British view of the status of the Aksai Chin tract north of the 1899 line at three moments in time, first in the light of the 1899 note, second in the discussions between the Indian and Home Governments in 1907 and in the Simla Convention map, and finally in a comparison of the British view with that view expressed by the Government of India since 1954.

*Map 11: Three stages in the evolution of the territorial status of Aksai Chin in British and Indian eyes*

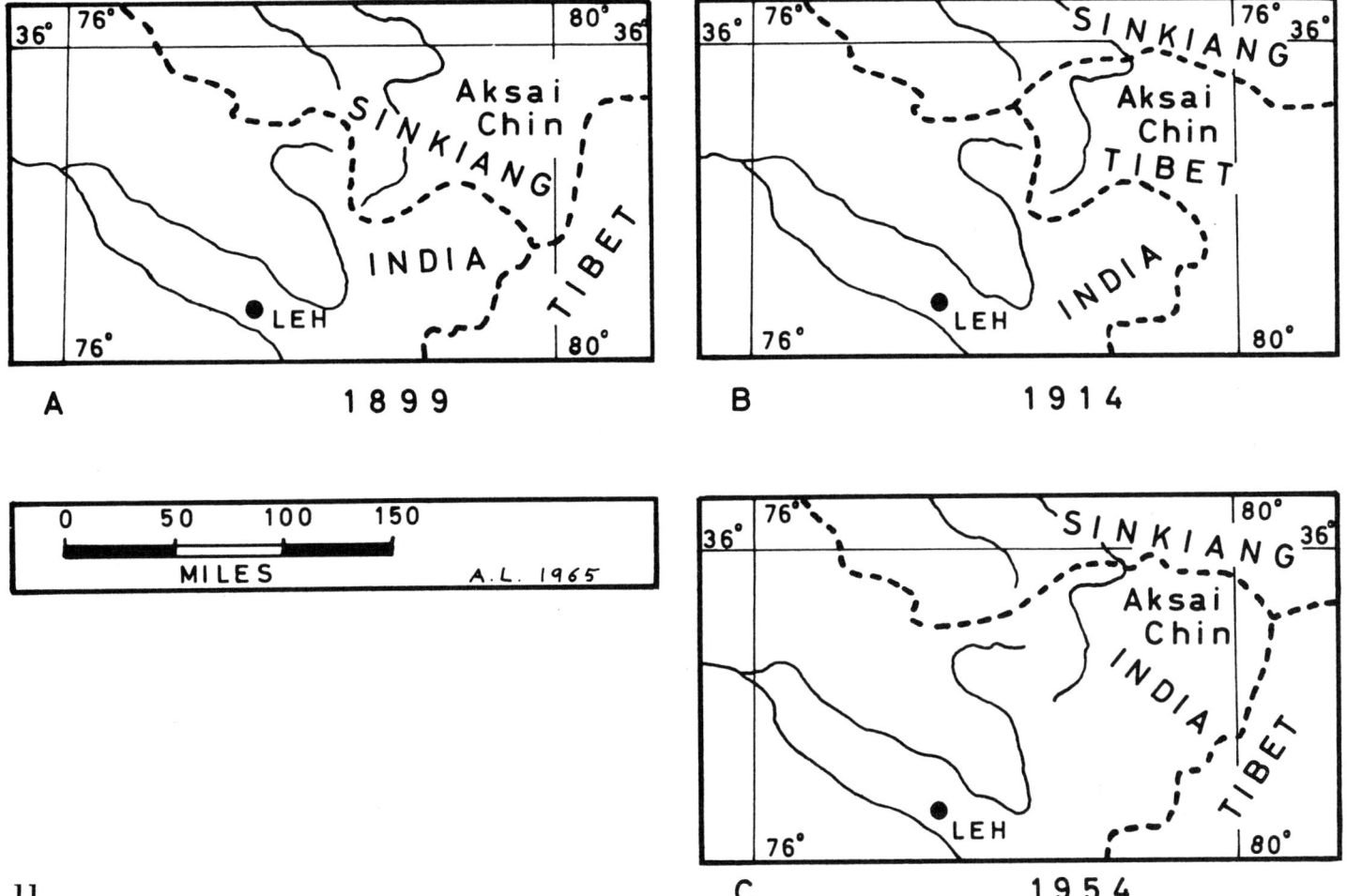

*Map 12* shows the evolution of the borders of northeastern Afghanistan in the latter part of the nineteenth century. The sector of the Russo-Afghan border between A and F was to some degree settled by direct Anglo-Russian diplomacy over the period 1869 to 1873. The line between F and G, Wood's Lake or Lake Victoria to the Pavalo-Schveikhovski Peak in the Pamirs, was settled by the Anglo-Russian boundary commission in 1895. The line marked B indicated what the Chinese up to 1895, indeed according to some Chinese writers up to the present, thought was the true western limit of their territory in Sinkiang; and, largely because of this Chinese attitude, the line marked C, starting just to the east of the Kara Kul Lake and running down to the Pavalo-Schveikhovski Peak at G, though after 1895 the *de facto* Sino-Russian border, has never been defined formally to this day. North of the Kara Kul Lake the Sino-Russian border was quite precisely defined in the 1880s, and from here until the Ili (which is a major problem spot) it is not subject to Chinese challenge so far as I am aware. The arrow marked E indicates the northeastern end of the Durand boundary negotiated between British India and Afghanistan in 1893. It will be seen that it terminates, too, at the Pavalo-Schveikhovski Peak, creating in the Wakhan tract a narrow strip of Afghan territory separating British India from the Russian Pamirs. The line marked D is the original 1899 boundary alignment between British India and China proposed in a note to the Chinese Government in March of 1899 by Sir Claude MacDonald. The interesting point to note here is that in this original form it runs north of the main Karakoram watershed to cross the Karachukur River and meet the Russian and Afghan borders at, once more, the Pavalo-Schveikhovski Peak which was a quadrijunction of Russian, Afghan, British, and Chinese territory. In the 1905 modification of the 1899 line, proposed by Lord Curzon and adopted unilaterally by the British, the western terminus of the 1899 line was in effect drawn back to stay with the main Karakoram watershed, thus creating a narrow stretch in the Pamirs of Sino-Afghan border and eliminating any point of contact whatsoever between British and Russian territory. In the 1960s this Sino-Afghan border has been confirmed by Peking.

*Map 12: The Russo-Afghan border along the Oxus and the Wakhan tract*

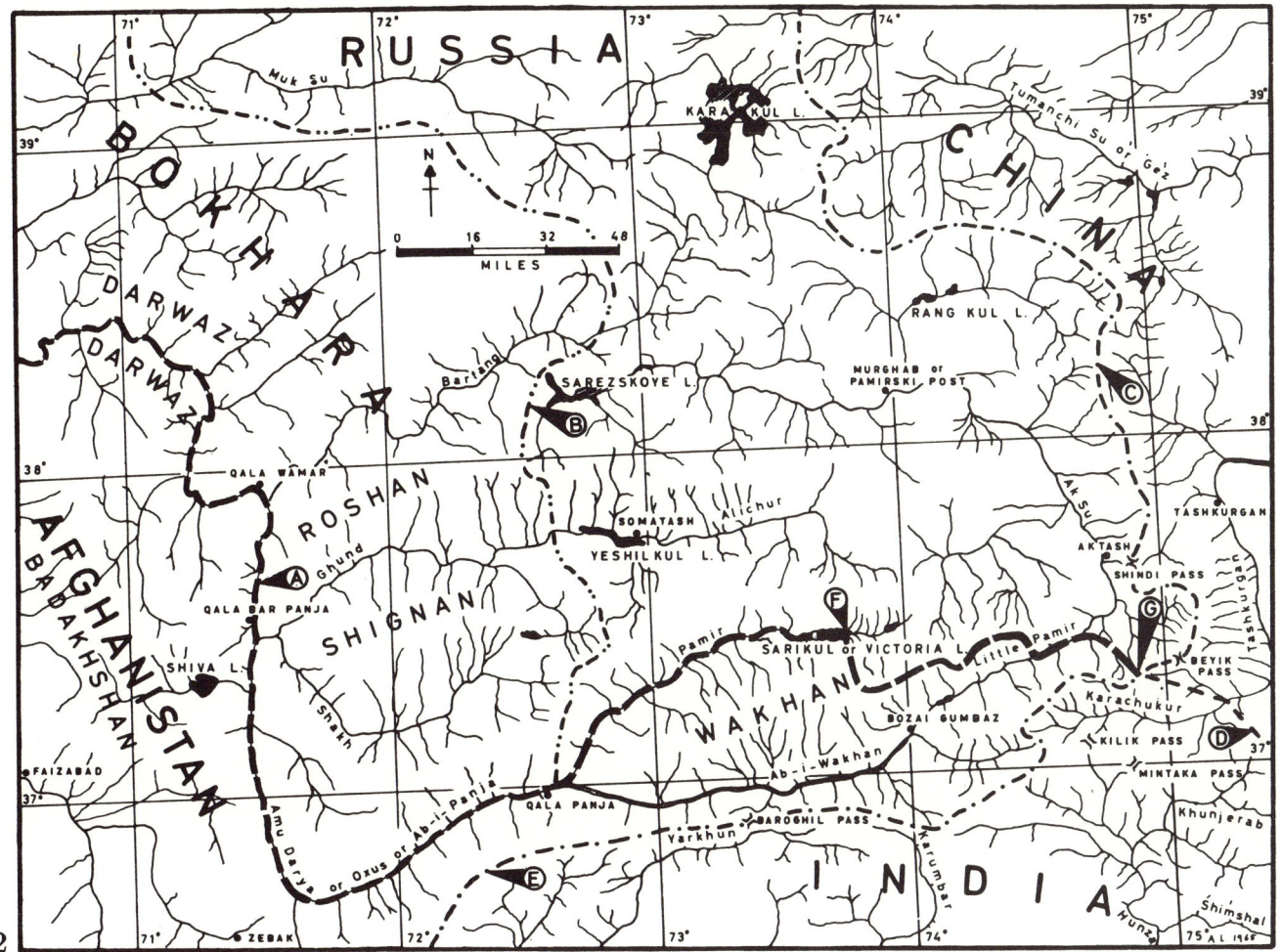

*Map 13* shows various boundary alignments, both proposed and actual, in the Pamirs and the western Karakoram. The legend included with this map is self explanatory. A point to notice is the region marked E, F and X which shows how modification of the 1899 line brought into being a short stretch of Sino-Afghan border. Another point to note is the very wide divergence in this region between the Ardagh type boundary, marked here H, and the 1899 line, F, with later modification G, this being the product of Lord Curzon's decision in 1905. It is also interesting to note how in such maps of the late British period as showed a boundary here at all there was a tendency to adopt a kind of compromise alignment between Ardagh and the 1899 proposals. This can be seen by following the line marked E.[3]

[3] The extreme western end of the line marked E, along the main Karakoram watershed, follows the same course as another modification in the 1899 line deriving from the 1905 period. Lord Curzon does not appear to have suggested informing the Chinese of this particular British withdrawal back from the Karachukur basin to the watershed.

*Map 13: Various boundary alignments in the Pamirs and the western Karakoram*

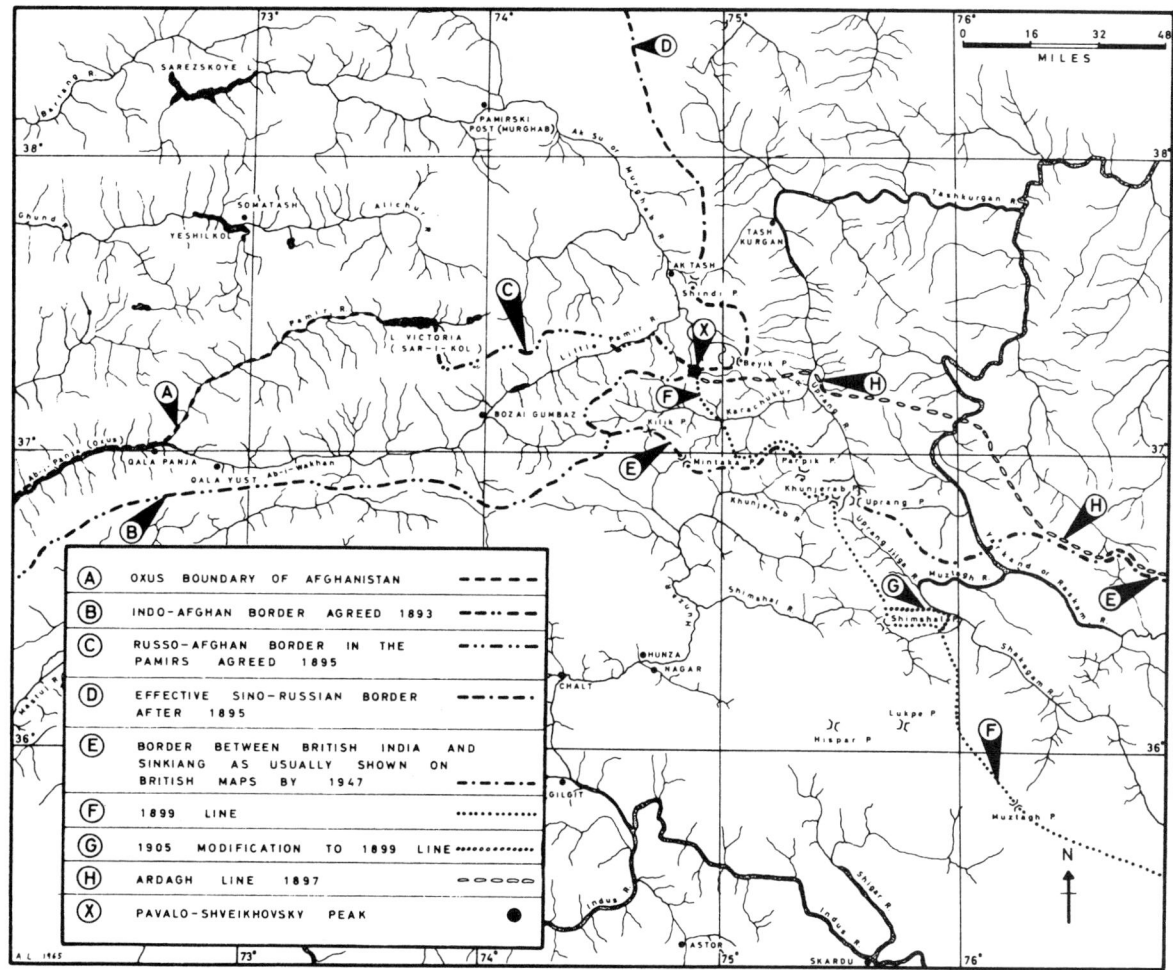

*Map 14* shows various boundary alignments in the eastern Karakoram and the Kunlun. Marked A is the 1899 line. It is interesting to note that in many places it coincides with the Chinese claim line advanced in the 1950s and that, where the 1899 line does diverge from the Chinese claim it is usually closer to that claim than to the claim raised by the Indian side. The Chinese claim is marked B. Much of the divergence between A and B to the west of the Muztagh Pass was resolved in the Sino-Pakistani agreement of March 1963. On this map the Indian claim, as based on official maps published from 1954 onwards and on the declarations of Indian officials in their discussions with their Chinese opposite numbers in 1960, is marked C. Except for a short tract immediately to the west of the Karakoram Pass, the intriguing feature of the Indian claim is that it agrees neither with the 1899 line nor with the boundary alignment, here marked D, which has been shown on many maps in the first half of the twentieth century including that 1:1,000,000 map produced by the U.S. Army in 1950 and, also, maps such as those contained in the *Times* and *Oxford Atlases* right up to the late 1950s. The Ardagh alignment, which was revived briefly by Lord Hardinge in 1912, is marked here as E. From the Yangi Pass in the Kunlun eastwards and then southwards it is interesting that the present Indian claim coincides with the Ardagh alignment and diverges dramatically from the 1899 line.

*Map 14: Various boundary alignments in the eastern Karakoram and the Kunlun*

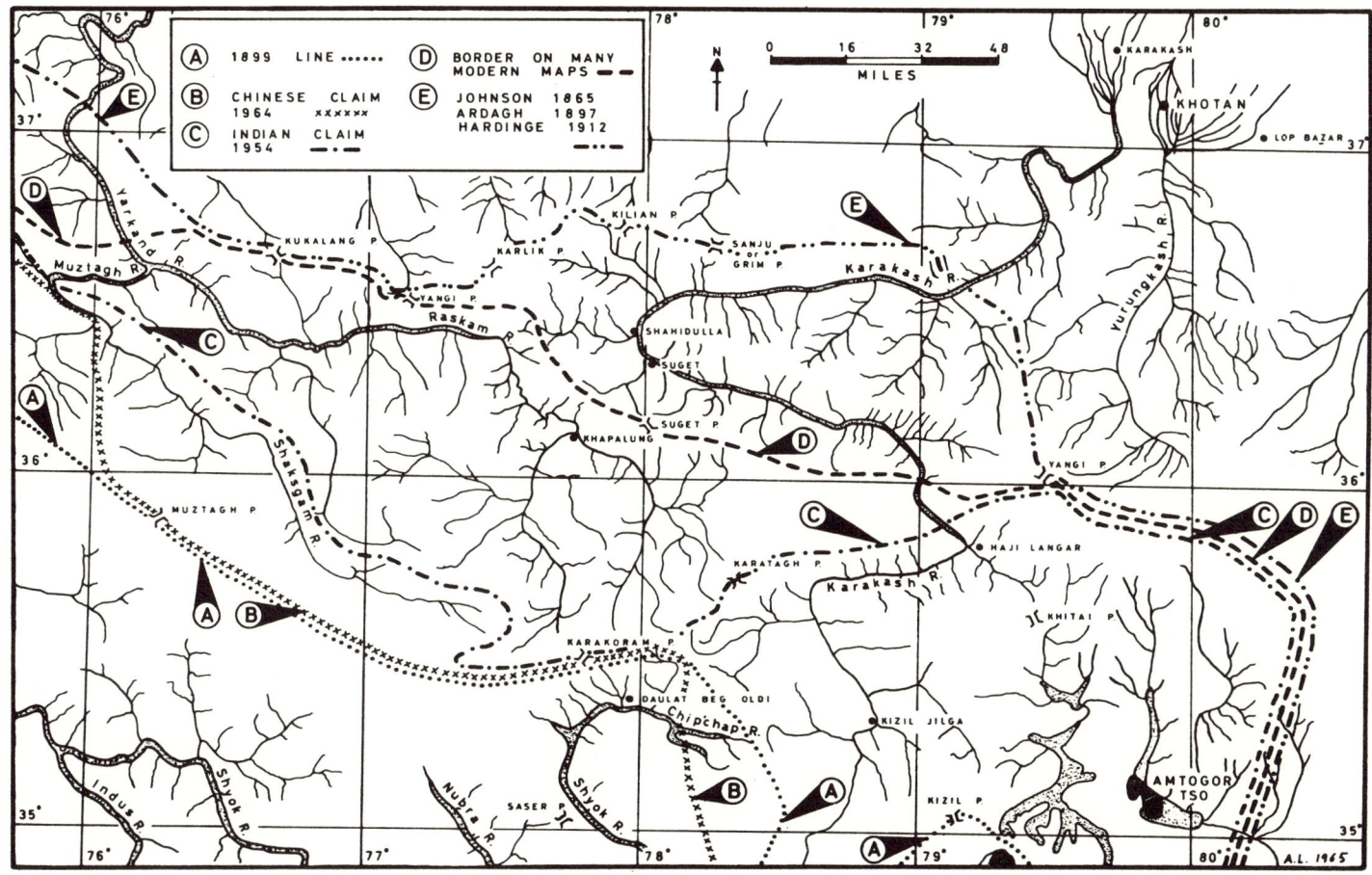

*Map 15* shows various boundary alignments proposed or claimed in the Aksai Chin region. Of considerable interest is the similarity of the present Chinese claim line to the boundary advocated in 1873 by T. Saunders, official cartographer to the India Office in London. Note also that Drew, who was actually carrying out survey work on behalf of the Maharaja of Kashmir, in his 1874 map concedes to China the entire Karakash basin. South of the Panggong Lake, Saunders, Drew, the proposers of the 1899 line, the present Government of India, and the Chinese disagree only on rather minor points when compared to the many thousands of square miles involved in their differences over Aksai Chin and Lingzitang.

*Map 15: Various boundary alignments in the Aksai Chin region*

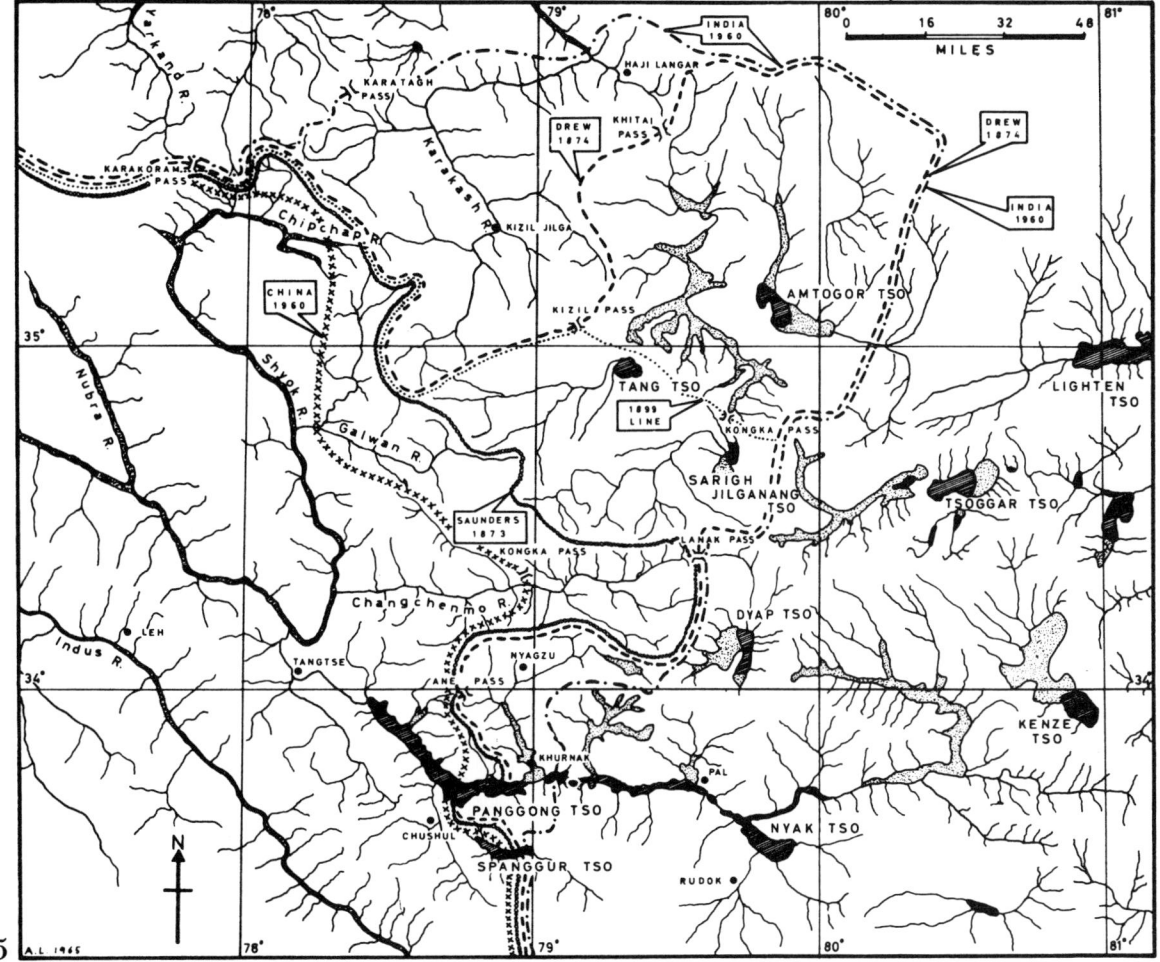

*Map 16* shows the location of Raskam and the Taghdumbash Pamir in relation to the main Karakoram watershed. The region which was of particular interest to the Mir of Hunza and which provided much of the raw material for the Raskam problem lay between the Shimshal Pass and the junction of the Uprang Jilga and Muztagh Rivers.

*Map 16: Raskam and the Taghdumbash Pamir*

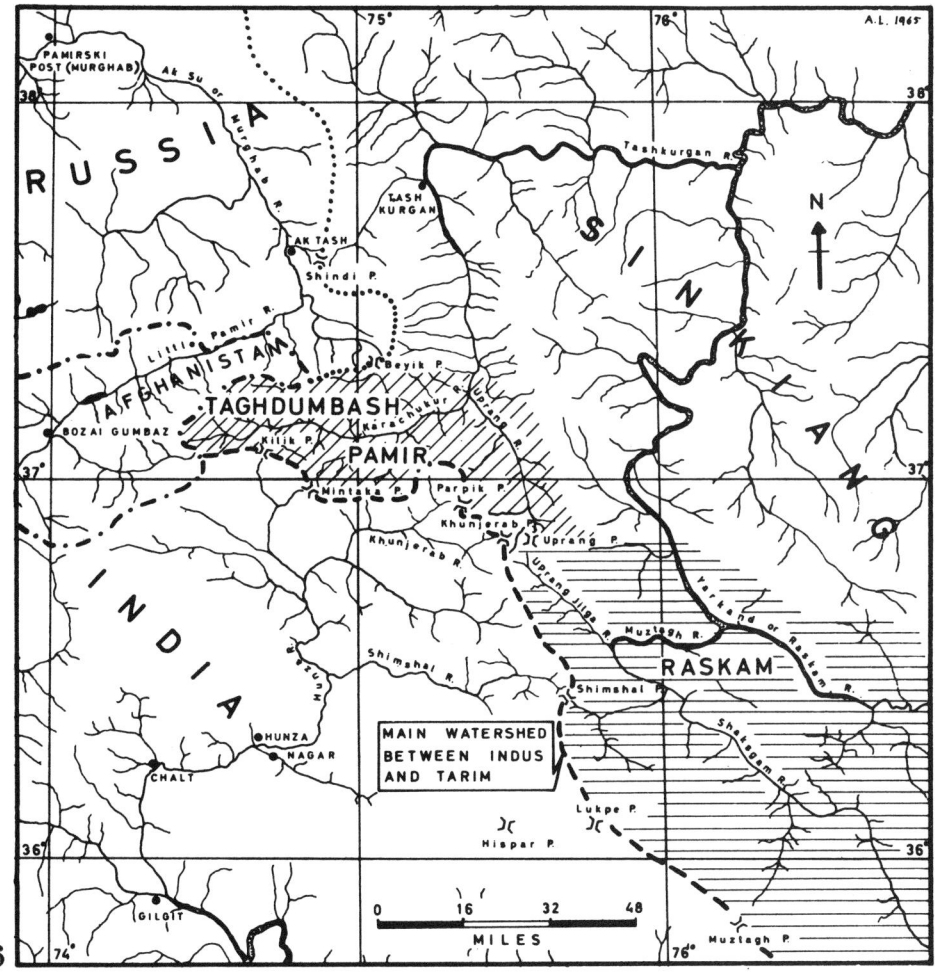

*Map 17* shows the western end of the 1899 line and the modifications made to it by Lord Curzon in 1905. It seems that, apart from the alteration in the Shimshal region, it was at this time that the decision was made to abandon British claims to any of the Karachukur basin north of the Mintaka and Kilik Passes over the Karakoram. This map also shows the boundary line settled by Sino-Pakistani agreement in March 1963. It is interesting to see that in the Shimshal region China agreed to Pakistani possession of considerably more territory (at least 700 square miles in all) than Lord Curzon had seen fit to seek beyond the watershed of the Karakoram in 1905.

*Map 17: The western end of the 1899 line with 1905 modifications and compared with the 1963 line agreed between China and Pakistan*

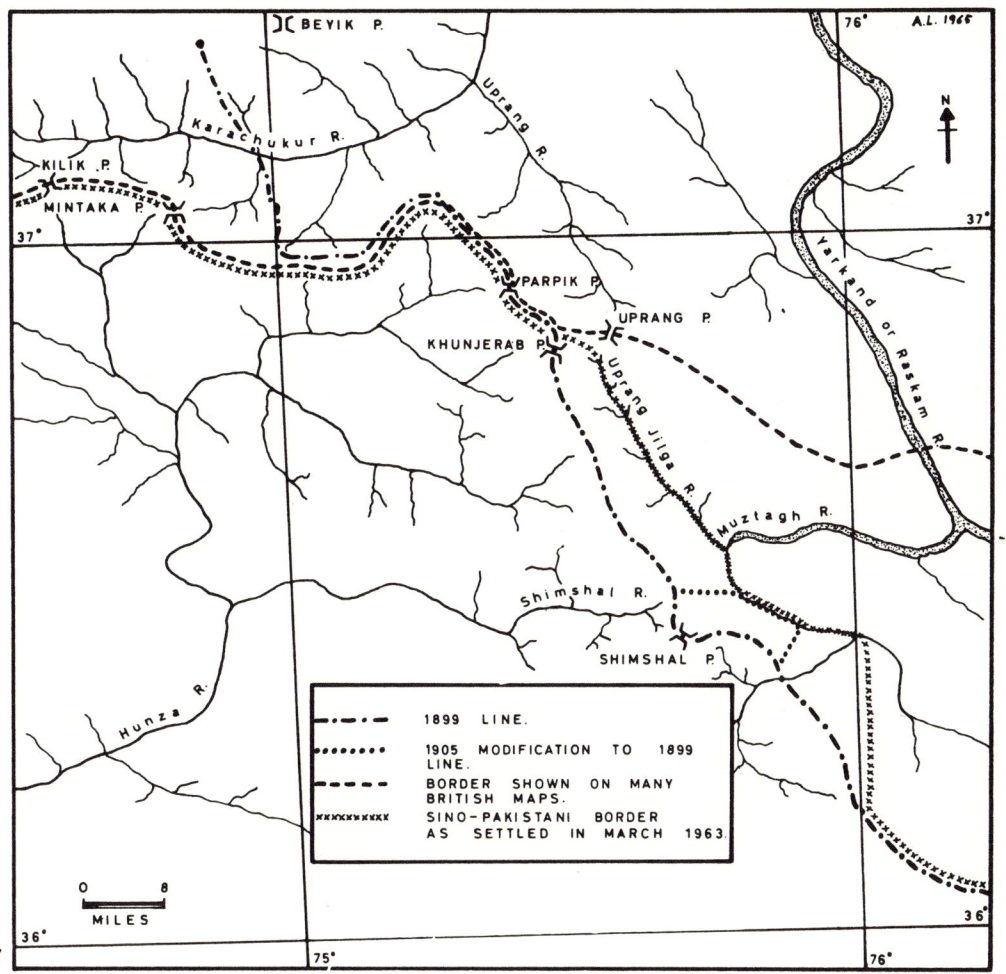

*Map 18* is reproduced here as an indication of how British ideas of the extent of Ladakh expanded during the middle of the nineteenth century. This particular map was drawn on the basis of official material to illustrate the boundaries of Ladakh shortly after the British had acquired, by virtue of their role in the creation of the State of Jammu and Kashmir, a direct interest in the region in 1846. By the time of the publication of the *Kashmir Atlas* in 1868 the eastern boundary of Ladakh had moved in more than 60 miles to the east to include features like Hanle and the Tso Morari Lake, here shown as external to Ladakh, and, one presumes, within Tibet.

*Map 18: A section of the north-eastern boundary of Ladakh as shown on a British map of the late 1840s*

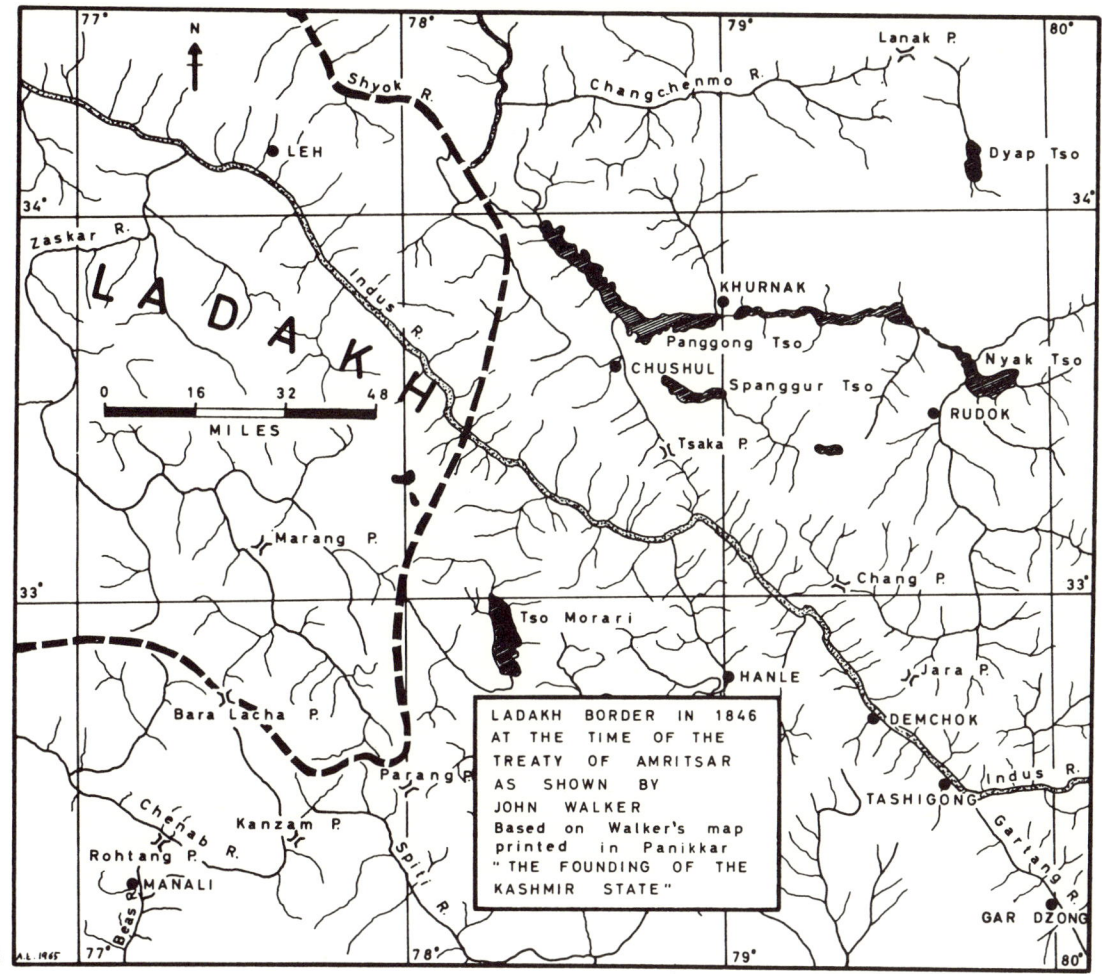

*Map 19* is a more detailed analysis than Map 3 of the relationship between the Indian and Chinese claims of recent times, the Chinese motor road between Sinkiang and Tibet and the 1899 line. In examining the course of the 1899 line one should bear in mind the considerations raised in connection with Map 7.

*Map 19: Detailed map of the Aksai Chin region showing location of modern Chinese and Indian claims, the Chinese road between Sinkiang and Tibet, and the 1899 line*

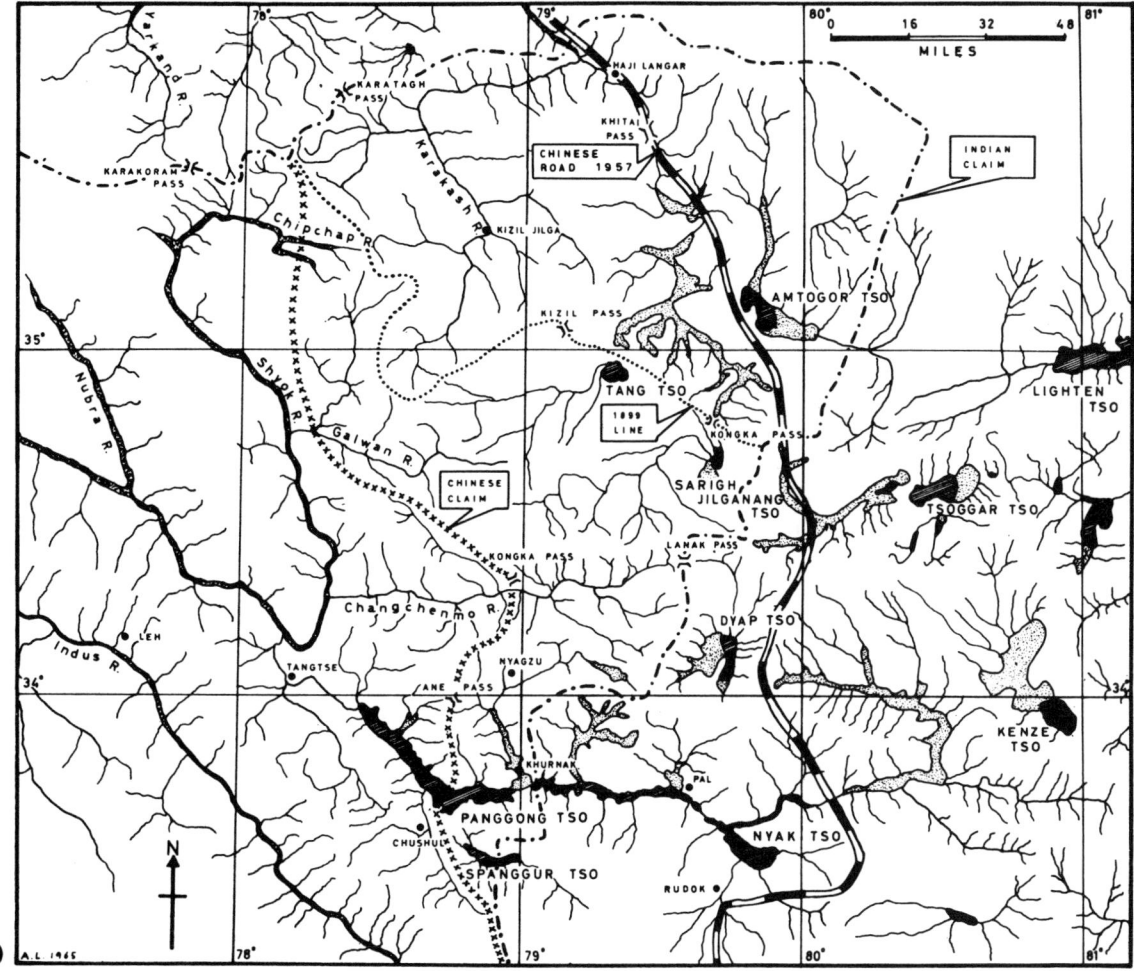

*Map 20* is designed to illustrate certain Indian departures since 1954 from the Kashmir boundaries often shown on maps in the British period. In the left hand map, in the region marked A, India has abandoned the shaded tract, which would have been British according to an Ardagh type alignment, without entirely accepting the alternative, the 1899 line. In the right hand map, in the regions marked B and C, India has claimed small tracts of territory in the area of Khurnak by the Panggong Lake and Demchok on the Indus which were never shown as being part of India on any British map which the author has ever seen. The essential point here, of course, is that the boundary which the Indians claimed in their discussions with China since the 1950s does not exactly coincide with any boundary alignment indicated by the British Government of India. Here, indeed, is a mystery.

*Map 20: Map showing some significant variations between Indian maps since 1954 and British maps relating to the boundaries along the Karakoram and the eastern side of Ladakh*

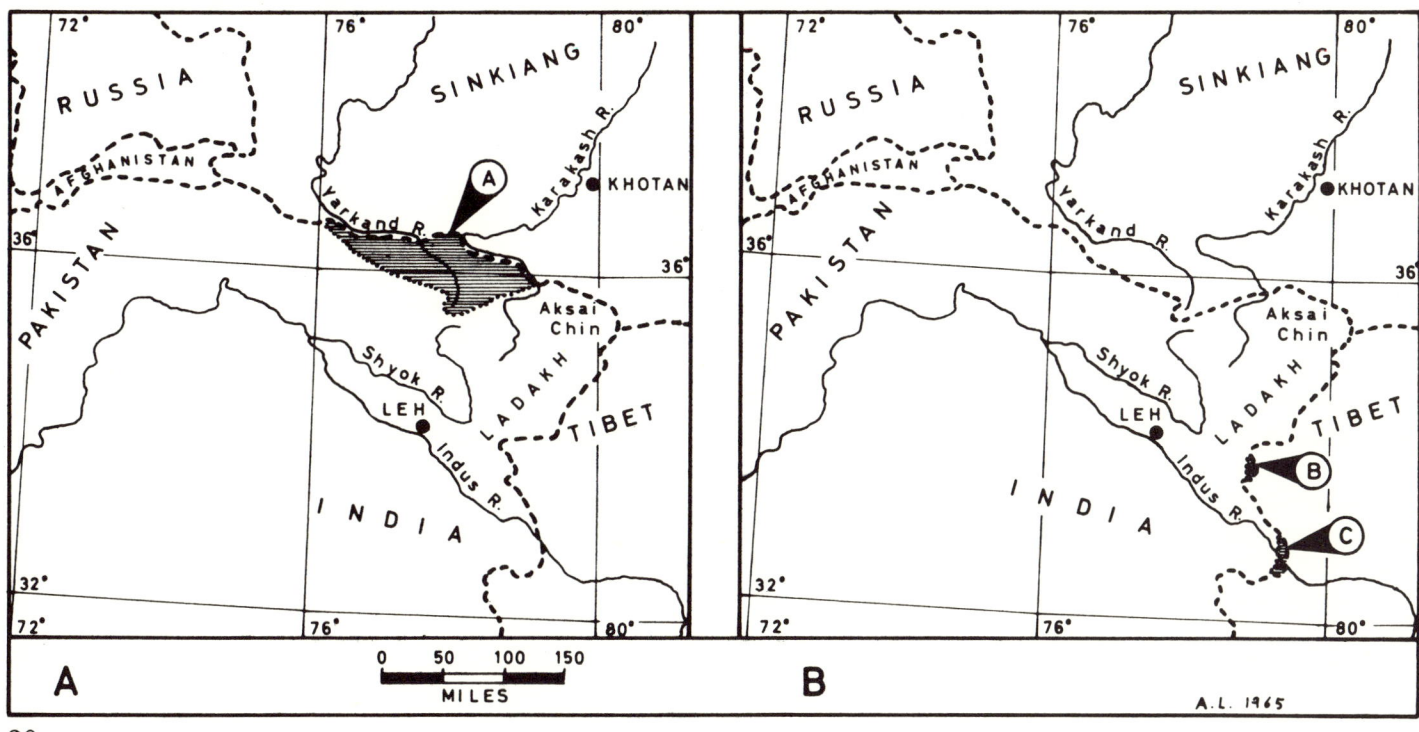

20

*Map 21.* This map, which is reproduced here last, is really where it all began. The tracing is of Johnson's own map, albeit slightly simplified, as it was reproduced in W. H. Johnson, 'Report on his journey to Ilchi, the capital of Khotan, in Chinese Tartary', *Journal of the Royal Geographical Society* XXXVII (1867). The subsequent influence of this map was profound. It dominated the section of the *Kashmir Atlas* of 1868 dealing with the northeastern corner of Ladakh; and from here onwards it has dominated Indian boundary views in this quarter. The main points to note on the present tracing are five. First, in the extreme southeast corner of Johnson's map Khurnak Fort, in recent years claimed by the Indian Republic, is shown as being well within the bounds of Tibet. Second, the streams feeding the Sarigh Jilganang basin from the east (see also **Map 7**) are shown to rise well to the east of the 80th meridian, an error of survey which was still undetected when the 1899 line was being formulated in 1898-99. Third, the boundary from the Yangi Pass on the Kunlun range turns abruptly northwards to take in much of the Karakash basin which even in 1865 certainly was in no way Kashmiri. The intention, here, no doubt, was to rationalise the presence of Kashmiri guards at Shahidulla on the Karakash at the point where that river is breaking through the northern foothills of the Tibetan massif into the Tarim basin. Fourth, the need to bring Shahidulla onto the Kashmiri side induced Johnson to place his boundary to the west of the Karakash along ridges far north of anything that the Indian Republic would claim today. The present point of apparently undisputed Sino-Indian contact here in this region now is the Karakoram Pass; but note how far north of this is Johnson's boundary line passing through the second Yangi Pass. Fifth, it is interesting to see that the northern parts of the Johnson map are even less accurate than those portions relating to Aksai Chin. The truth is that the precise topography of the northern edges of the Kunlun and its adjacent ranges was not worked out until well on in the twentieth century. Meanwhile the fossil remains of earlier surveys have survived, like the hind legs of a whale, in many a modern map.

*Map 21: Johnson's map of the northern frontier of Kashmir, based on his journey to Khotan in 1865*

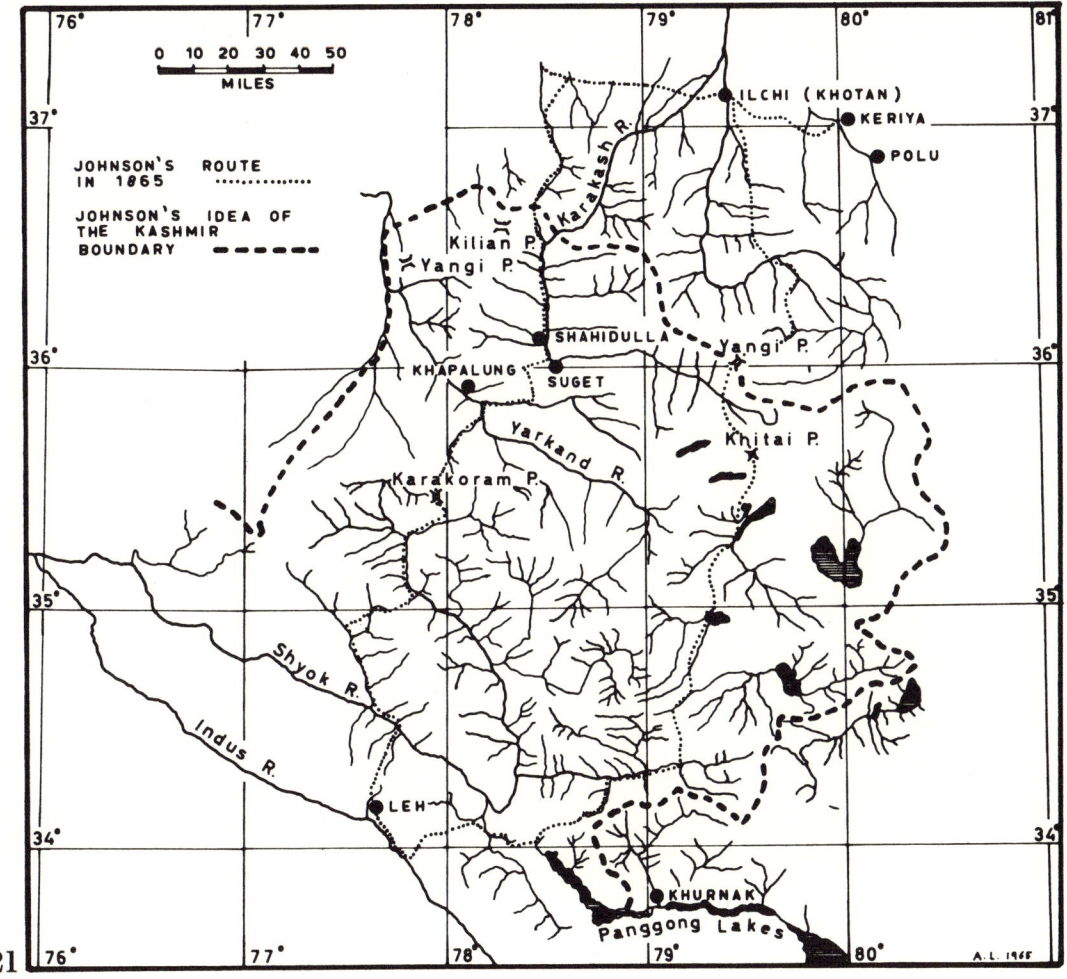

***The Sino-Indian Border in Ladakh***

The typeface is Monotype Imprint.
The book was printed by offset lithography by Kingsport Press, Inc.,
on Warren's University Text, a paper of extraordinary longevity,
especially watermarked with the emblem of the
University of South Carolina Press,
and bound at Kingsport Press, Inc.

ET 30889